AF531501

Global Agricultural Innovations
Seeds of Progress

About the Editors

Maitreyee Tripathy is currently pursuing her Doctoral degree in the Department of Agricultural Extension Education from Odisha University of Agriculture and Technology (OUAT), Bhubaneswar with ICSSR (Indian Council of Social Science Research) Doctoral Fellowship. She had completed her Master's degree in the Department of Agricultural Extension from Visva-Bharati University, Santiniketan, West Bengal with Junior Research Fellowship (JRF-ICAR) in 2020. She has qualified both UGC-NET and ICAR-NET in 2019 and 2021 respectively. She was also awarded PGDJMC (Post Graduate Diploma in Journalism and Mass Communication) from BJB Junior College, Bhubaneswar under Odisha State Open University (OSOU) in 2022. She has to her credit several research and review papers published in various reputed national and international UGC Care and Scopus Indexed Journals, book chapters, popular articles in national and international magazines, technical bulletins and other extension publications. She has got several best paper presentation awards in various national and international conferences. She has authored two textbooks; Extension Landscape and Programme Evaluation and Impact Assessment, which has been published in prestigious outlets and is crafted in accordance with the restructured and revised syllabi of ICAR-PG.

Guru Prasad Satapathy is currently pursuing Ph.D. degree in the Department of Agricultural Extension Education from Odisha University of Agriculture and Technology (OUAT), Bhubaneswar with UGC-SRF (Senior Research Fellowship). He has qualified UGC-NET with JRF, ICAR-NET and ICAR-SRF in 2019, 2021 and 2020 respectively. He had completed his Master's degree in the Department of Agricultural Extension Education from University of Agricultural Science, Dharwad, Karnataka with Junior Research Fellowship (JRF-ICAR) in 2020. He is a prolific publisher of several research and review papers in various reputed national and international UGC Care and Scopus Indexed Journals, book chapters, popular articles in national and international magazines, technical bulletins and other extension publications. He has written two textbooks; Extension Landscape and Programme Evaluation and Impact Assessment aligned with the restructured ICAR-PG syllabi, published in prestigious outlets. He has been recognized for his outstanding research presentations in various national and international conferences.

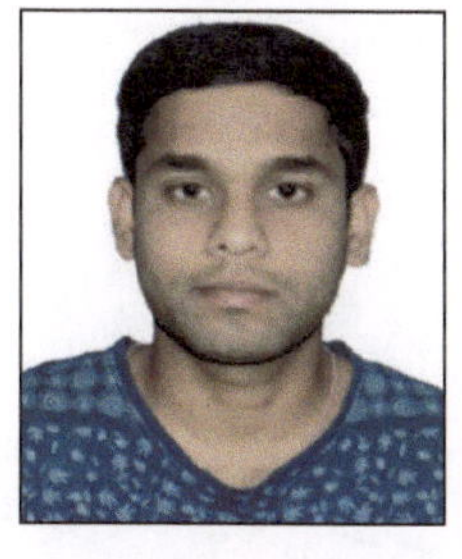

Debabrata Swain is currently working as an Assistant Professor in Department of Agricultural Economics, Faculty of Agricultural Sciences in Siksha "O" Anusandhan University, Bhubaneswar. He had completed his Ph.D. degree in the Department of Agricultural Economics from Chandra Sekhar Azad University of Agriculture and Technology (CSAUA&T), Kanpur, Uttar Pradesh with ICAR-SRF (Senior Research Fellowship) in 2023. He has qualified, ICAR-NET and ICAR-SRF in, 2021 and 2020 respectively. He had completed his Master's degree in the Department of Agricultural Economics from Sam Higginbottom University of Agriculture, Technology and Sciences, Prayagraj, Uttar Pradesh with National Talent Scholarship (NTS-ICAR) in 2020. He is a prolific publisher of several research and review papers in various reputed national and international UGC Care and Scopus Indexed Journals, book chapters, popular articles in national and international magazines, technical bulletins and other Economics publications. He has been recognized for his outstanding research presentations in various national and international conferences.

Global Agricultural Innovations Seeds of Progress

Maitreyee Tripathy
Odisha University of Agriculture and Technology
Bhubaneswar-751003
Odisha, India

Guru Prasad Satapathy
Odisha University of Agriculture and Technology
Bhubaneswar-751003
Odisha, India

Debabrata Swain
Assistant Professor
Department of Agricultural Economics
'SOA' Deemed to be University
Bhubaneswar

FU 75, Pitam Pura
New Delhi 110034
publishmywork23@gmail.com
Mob. 91-8447075807

ISBN: 978-93-61346-85-9

Preface

In the annals of human history, few endeavors have been as pivotal and transformative as agriculture. It is the bedrock upon which civilizations have flourished, sustenance has been secured, and societies have evolved. Yet, in the tapestry of our progress, the threads of innovation in agriculture stand out as the brightest, weaving a story of resilience, adaptation, and the unyielding pursuit of feeding a growing world. "Global Agricultural Innovations Seeds of Progress" celebrates this narrative, delving into the crucial importance of agricultural innovations. From ancient practices rooted in tradition to cutting-edge technologies shaping our future, this book serves as a testament to the inexorable drive of humanity to cultivate progress, nourishing not just crops but the very fabric of our existence.

To the academic community, this book stands as an invaluable testament to the perpetual evolution and it is a compendium that underscores the pivotal role of agriculture in the academic sphere and is important for graduate and postgraduate and doctoral studies. It illuminates the corridors of learning, inviting scholars, researchers, and educators to delve deeper into the profound impact and intricate tapestry of innovations within the agricultural domain. This book serves as a beacon, guiding academia through the fertile fields of exploration, inviting discourse, and fostering a deeper understanding of the crucial interplay between innovation, sustainability, and global food security. Its pages hold the keys to unlocking new paradigms, nurturing fertile ground for scholarly pursuits, and inspiring the next generation of agricultural leaders and thinkers.

The core areas like Sustainable Farming Practices, Strategic Approaches to Agricultural Marketing, Empowering Youth in Agriculture, Regenerative Agriculture, Challenges and Opportunities in Global Food Security, Role of Women in Agriculture, Technology Advancements and Digital Transformation in Extension, etc. have been described in simple understandable languages for readers with proper examples.

This book aims to provide agriculturists as a comprehensive resource for their work. It covers a wide range of relevant topics, including newer areas and concepts. The book will also be of interest to researchers, students, teachers, and other professionals who work in the fields of agriculture and social science.

Editors

Preface

Contents

1

Sustainable Farming Practices Nurturing the Earth for Future Generations

S.P. Monalisa

Seed Science and Technology, Faculty of Agricultural Sciences, 'SOA' Bhubaneswar, Odisha

ABSTRACT

India's agricultural landscape showcases a dynamic blend of ancient wisdom and contemporary innovations in sustainable farming practices. From the Indus Valley Civilization's sophisticated irrigation systems to Ayurveda's holistic principles influencing agriculture, the nation's agricultural heritage underscores a deep-rooted connection with the land. The exponential growth of organic farming, water conservation initiatives inspired by traditional methods, and efforts to preserve crop diversity and indigenous seeds reflect the diverse tapestry of sustainable practices. However, challenges persist—land degradation, economic viability, and water scarcity demand holistic solutions. Despite these hurdles, India's future in sustainable farming appears promising, driven by governmental support, technological advancements, and a rising tide of consumer awareness. This abstract encapsulates India's journey—a continuous commitment to harmonize tradition with innovation, fostering a sustainable agricultural legacy for a prosperous future.

Keywords: *Sustainable Agriculture, Traditional Wisdom, Organic Farming, Holistic Practices*

Introduction

Sustainable farming, rooted in the harmonious interaction between nature and agriculture, stands as a beacon of hope for India's agricultural landscape, paving the way for a resilient and ecologically balanced future. In a world increasingly confronted by environmental challenges, the urgency to adopt sustainable farming practices has become paramount, and India, with its rich agricultural heritage, exemplifies a tapestry of wisdom and innovation in this regard.For millennia, India's agrarian communities have cultivated a deep relationship with the land, inheriting traditional farming practices that fostered harmony with nature. From the ancient techniques of the Indus Valley Civilization to the holistic principles of Ayurveda influencing farming methods, the country's agricultural history is a repository of sustainable wisdom. These practices, ingrained in the cultural fabric, not only sustained livelihoods but also preserved the ecological equilibrium.

In recent times, a resurgence of interest in organic farming has emerged, marking a shift towards ecologically sensitive agriculture. States like Sikkim have achieved remarkable milestones by becoming entirely organic, setting a precedent for the nation. This movement towards organic practices not only promotes healthier produce but also revitalizes soil fertility and safeguards biodiversity.Moreover, India's embrace of agroforestry and permaculture signifies a shift towards more integrated and sustainable farming systems. Initiatives like Chetna Organic in Maharashtra demonstrate the power of harmonizing agriculture with the natural landscape, fostering resilience and diversity within farming ecosystems.

Water scarcity poses a significant challenge to agriculture, especially in a country as diverse as India. However, the revival of traditional water harvesting techniques alongside modern innovations like drip irrigation showcases a blended approach, ensuring efficient water usage and conservation.

Despite these strides, challenges persist. Issues such as declining soil health, economic viability, and the need for widespread adoption of sustainable practices demand immediate attention. Governmental initiatives like the Pradhan Mantri Fasal Bima Yojana aim to support farmers, yet gaps exist in implementation and accessibility.

Definition and Importance of Sustainable Farming

1. Definition of Sustainable Farming

- Sustainable farming refers to agricultural practices that aim to meet present-day food needs without compromising the ability of future generations to meet their own needs.
- It involves cultivating the land in a manner that preserves and enhances environmental quality, economic viability, and social equity.

2. Importance of Sustainable Farming

- **Environmental Preservation**: It prioritizes the conservation of natural resources, such as soil, water, and biodiversity, ensuring their availability for future agricultural use.
- **Economic Viability**: Sustainable farming practices often lead to improved farm profitability in the long term by reducing input costs, enhancing soil fertility, and diversifying income sources.

- **Climate Resilience**: By adopting techniques that reduce greenhouse gas emissions and sequester carbon, sustainable farming helps mitigate climate change effects on agriculture.
- **Healthier Food Production**: It promotes the production of nutritious and safe food by minimizing the use of synthetic chemicals, pesticides, and fertilizers.
- **Community and Social Equity**: Sustainable farming fosters stronger community ties, supports local economies, and enhances social equity by ensuring fair treatment and opportunities for farmers.

3. Indian Examples of Sustainable Farming

- **Organic Farming Initiatives**: Increasing adoption of organic farming methods in various states like Sikkim, Karnataka, and Himachal Pradesh exemplifies India's commitment to sustainable agriculture.
- **Agroforestry Practices**: Instances of integrating trees within farming systems, prevalent in states like Tamil Nadu and Kerala, showcase sustainable land use and diversified income sources.
- **Water Conservation Techniques**: Ancient water harvesting methods in Rajasthan and modern innovations in drip irrigation across Maharashtra exhibit India's efforts towards sustainable water management in agriculture.
- **Seed Banks and Crop Diversity Conservation**: Initiatives like Navdanya's seed bank in Uttarakhand emphasize the preservation of indigenous seed varieties, ensuring crop diversity and resilience.

4. Future Prospects

- The adoption of technology, precision agriculture, and the scaling up of successful sustainable models are key to addressing future challenges.
- Government support and policies that incentivize and promote sustainable farming practices can further catalyze the transition towards a more sustainable agricultural landscape in India.

B. Need for Sustainable Farming in India

I. Environmental Degradation

- **Soil Health**: India faces severe soil degradation due to intensive farming practices, erosion, and chemical-heavy agriculture, threatening long-term agricultural productivity.
- **Water Scarcity**: With water stress affecting many regions, sustainable farming methods are essential to conserve water resources and ensure their availability for agriculture.

2. Climate Change Vulnerability

- **Erratic Weather Patterns**: Increasingly unpredictable weather patterns, including droughts and floods, necessitate resilient farming practices that can adapt to and mitigate the effects of climate change.
- **Mitigating Greenhouse Gas Emissions**: Agriculture contributes significantly to greenhouse gas emissions. Sustainable practices can help reduce emissions and enhance carbon sequestration.

3. Smallholder Farmer Livelihoods

- **Economic Viability**: Many smallholder farmers struggle with economic viability due to rising input costs, low productivity, and market volatility. Sustainable methods offer cost-effective alternatives and diversified income sources.
- **Social Equity**: Promoting sustainable practices ensures fair treatment and opportunities for smallholder farmers, empowering them to improve their livelihoods.

4. Health and Food Security

- **Chemical-Free Food Production**: Excessive use of chemical fertilizers and pesticides poses health risks for consumers and farmers. Sustainable farming ensures the production of healthier and safer food.
- **Nutritional Security**: Diverse, sustainable farming practices enhance crop diversity and nutritional value, contributing to better food security for the population.

5. Biodiversity Preservation

- **Loss of Biodiversity**: Monoculture and intensive farming practices contribute to the loss of indigenous crop varieties and biodiversity. Sustainable farming methods prioritize preserving diverse plant species, crucial for resilience against pests and diseases.

6. Governmental and Global Imperatives

- **Policy Support**: Aligning with global sustainability goals, India needs robust policies and governmental support to promote and incentivize sustainable farming practices.
- **International Commitments**: As a signatory to global agreements like the Paris Agreement and Sustainable Development Goals (SDGs), India has committed to sustainable agricultural practices.

II. Traditional Indian Farming Techniques

A. Ancient Methods: Examples from Indus Valley Civilization

1. Sophisticated Irrigation Systems:

- **Canal Networks**: The Indus Valley Civilization, notably Mohenjo-Daro and Harappa, showcased an advanced understanding of hydraulics with an intricate network of canals and drainage systems. These systems facilitated controlled water distribution for agricultural purposes.

2. Crop Cultivation Practices

- **Crop Rotation**: Archaeological evidence suggests that farmers practiced crop rotation to maintain soil fertility and prevent soil depletion. This method involved alternating crops in a systematic pattern over time.
- **Diverse Agricultural Produce**: The Indus Valley people cultivated a wide variety of crops, including wheat, barley, pulses, and cotton, displaying a diverse agricultural landscape.

3. Terraced Farming

- **Hillside Agriculture**: In certain regions with varying topography, terraced farming was evident. This technique involved creating stepped or layered fields on slopes, minimizing soil erosion and maximizing arable land.

4. Livestock Integration:

- **Animal Husbandry**: Evidence suggests the integration of livestock, particularly cattle, in agricultural practices. Animals were used for plowing fields, and their dung was utilized as a natural fertilizer.

5. Natural Resource Management:

- **Waste Management**: The civilization displayed efficient waste management systems, using organic waste and biomass as resources for agriculture. This practice contributed to soil enrichment and fertility.

6. Sustainability Principles:

- **Harmony with Nature**: The farming techniques of the Indus Valley Civilization emphasized a symbiotic relationship with the environment, focusing on sustainable practices to ensure long-term agricultural productivity without degrading the land.

B. Indigenous Knowledge: Role of Ayurveda in Farming

1. Foundations of Ayurvedic Agriculture:

- **Holistic Principles**: Ayurveda, an ancient Indian system of medicine, extends its holistic approach to agriculture, viewing farming as an interconnected system.
- **Tridosha Theory**: Similar to its application in healthcare, Ayurveda applies the tridosha theory (Vata, Pitta, Kapha) to agricultural practices, emphasizing balance and harmony for optimal crop growth.

2. Natural Farming Practices:

- **Herbal Solutions**: Ayurvedic principles promote the use of herbal concoctions and natural extracts for pest control and soil enrichment. Examples include neem-based pesticides and cow urine formulations.

- **Compost and Soil Enrichment**: Ayurvedic farming emphasizes the use of organic compost, such as vermicompost and herbal compost, to enhance soil fertility and promote plant health.

3. Crop-Disease Management:

- **Crop Protection**: Ayurvedic texts suggest various methods to protect crops from diseases, including the use of herbal preparations and natural biocides to prevent and manage plant ailments.
- **Crop Rotation and Diversity**: Ayurvedic farming advocates crop rotation and the cultivation of diverse crops to prevent disease outbreaks and maintain soil vitality.

4. Seasonal and Lunar Influence:

- **Timing of Planting**: Ayurvedic farming emphasizes planting and harvesting based on lunar cycles and seasonal variations, aligning agricultural activities with natural rhythms believed to optimize plant growth.

5. Promotion of Biodiversity:

- **Preservation of Native Varieties**: Ayurvedic agriculture encourages the preservation and cultivation of native and indigenous crop varieties, respecting their inherent qualities and benefits.

6. Spiritual and Ethical Dimensions:

- **Respect for Nature**: Ayurvedic farming principles stem from a deep-rooted respect for nature and the belief in the interconnectedness of all living beings, fostering a sense of responsibility towards the environment.

III. Organic Farming in India

A. Growth of Organic Farming: Trends and Statistics

1. Rapid Expansion:

- **Increasing Adoption**: Over the last decade, India has witnessed a significant surge in organic farming practices across various states.
- **Statistics**: According to government data, the area under organic certification has been steadily increasing, with several million hectares dedicated to organic cultivation.

2. State-Level Initiatives:

- **Sikkim's Remarkable Achievement**: Sikkim became the first fully organic state in India, transitioning all its agriculture to organic methods, setting a precedent for other states.
- **State Policies**: States like Himachal Pradesh, Kerala, and Karnataka have formulated policies and allocated resources to promote organic farming.

3. Certification and Export:

- **Certification Bodies**: Various agencies, both governmental and private, offer organic certification, ensuring adherence to organic standards.

- **Export Market**: India has emerged as a significant exporter of organic produce, catering to global demands for organic products, including spices, tea, coffee, and cereals.

4. Farmer Participation and Support:

- **Increasing Farmer Interest**: Many farmers are voluntarily shifting to organic practices due to increased awareness of health and environmental benefits.
- **Government Support**: Programs like Paramparagat Krishi Vikas Yojana (PKVY) provide financial support and training to farmers adopting organic methods.

5. Consumer Awareness and Demand:

- **Urban Market Demand**: Growing health-consciousness among urban consumers has fueled the demand for organic products, encouraging the expansion of organic farming.
- **Retail Availability**: Organic produce is increasingly available in supermarkets and specialized organic stores, catering to the rising demand.

6. Challenges and Opportunities:

- **Scaling-Up Challenges**: While organic farming is growing, challenges remain in scaling up production to meet increasing demand.
- **Education and Training**: Opportunities exist to enhance education and training for farmers to ensure successful adoption and maintenance of organic practices.

B. Case Study: Sikkim's Transition to Fully Organic Farming State

1. Policy Framework:

- **Sikkim's Vision**: In 2003, Sikkim set the ambitious goal of becoming entirely organic, envisioning a state free from chemical pesticides and fertilizers.
- **Government Commitment**: The state government implemented policies and allocated resources to support farmers in transitioning to organic practices.

2. Systematic Phased Approach

- **Phase-wise Implementation**: Sikkim's transition occurred in phases, initially focusing on converting individual farms and gradually expanding to cover the entire state.
- **Farmer Training**: Extensive training programs and workshops were conducted to educate farmers about organic farming techniques and sustainable practices.

3. Community Participation and Incentives:

- **Community Engagement**: The success of Sikkim's transition relied on active involvement and cooperation from farmers, NGOs, and local communities.
- **Financial Support**: The state government provided subsidies, incentives, and financial aid to encourage and support farmers during the transition period.

4. Certification and Quality Assurance

- **Certification Process**: Sikkim collaborated with certification agencies to ensure adherence to organic standards and facilitate the certification of organic produce.
- **Quality Assurance**: Rigorous monitoring and evaluation systems were established to maintain the quality and integrity of organic farming practices.

5. Economic and Environmental Impact:

- **Economic Viability**: Contrary to skepticism, the transition enhanced economic viability for farmers by reducing input costs and increasing market access for organic produce.
- **Environmental Benefits**: The shift eliminated the use of chemical fertilizers and pesticides, benefiting soil health, biodiversity, and water quality.

6. Global Recognition and Inspiration:

- **International Acclaim**: Sikkim's achievement gained global recognition, positioning the state as a model for sustainable agriculture worldwide.
- **Inspiration for Others**: The success of Sikkim's transition inspired other Indian states and countries globally to consider and implement similar organic farming initiatives.

V. Water Conservation Techniques

1. Traditional Water Harvesting Methods

- **Johads and Talabs**: Rajasthan showcases the effectiveness of traditional water harvesting structures like johads (earthen check dams) and talabs (ponds), which trap rainwater and recharge groundwater.
- **Ahar-Pyne System**: Used in Bihar, this ancient method involves interconnected ponds (ahars) and channels (pynes) for efficient water distribution and storage.

2. Modern Irrigation Technologies

- **Drip Irrigation**: Widely adopted in states like Maharashtra and Karnataka, drip irrigation minimizes water wastage by delivering precise amounts of water directly to the plant roots.
- **Sprinkler Systems**: Utilized in areas like Punjab and Haryana, sprinkler systems evenly distribute water, reducing water loss through evaporation.

3. Community-Led Water Conservation Initiatives

- **Tamil Nadu's Tank Restoration**: Restoration and desilting of traditional irrigation tanks (kulams) in Tamil Nadu have revived water sources, benefiting agriculture and replenishing groundwater levels.
- **Watershed Management Projects**: Various states implement watershed management projects involving contour trenches and bunds, preventing soil erosion and allowing rainwater to percolate into the soil.

4. Rainwater Harvesting Techniques

- **Rooftop Rainwater Harvesting**: Adopted in urban and rural areas across India, this technique collects rainwater from rooftops into storage tanks for domestic and agricultural use.
- **Percolation Pits**: Constructed in regions like Gujarat and Maharashtra, percolation pits enable rainwater to seep into the ground, recharging aquifers and augmenting groundwater levels.

5. Governmental Initiatives

- **Pradhan Mantri Krishi Sinchayee Yojana (PMKSY)**: This scheme focuses on improving irrigation efficiency and water use in agriculture, aiming to achieve "Har Khet Ko Pani" (Water to Every Field).
- **Jal Shakti Abhiyan**: Launched to address water scarcity, the campaign emphasizes water conservation, rainwater harvesting, and promoting efficient water use.

6. Challenges and Future Directions

- **Sustainable Water Management**: Balancing water demand with supply remains crucial, necessitating a holistic approach that integrates traditional wisdom with modern technologies.
- **Awareness and Participation**: Encouraging community involvement and raising awareness about the importance of water conservation is pivotal for the sustained success of these initiatives.

VI. Crop Diversity and Seed Preservation

1. Importance of Crop Diversity

- **Resilience to Climate Variability**: Diverse crops offer resilience against climatic fluctuations, safeguarding against crop failures and ensuring food security.
- **Nutritional Diversity**: Different crops provide a variety of nutrients, contributing to a balanced and diverse diet, crucial for overall health.

2. Seed Banks and Conservation Efforts

- **Navdanya Movement**: Led by Vandana Shiva, Navdanya promotes seed sovereignty and conservation of native seed varieties, preserving traditional knowledge and biodiversity.

- **National Gene Banks**: Institutions like the National Bureau of Plant Genetic Resources (NBPGR) maintain extensive seed banks, conserving diverse crop germplasm.

3. Indigenous Seed Saving Practices

- **Farmers' Role**: Traditional farming communities actively participate in seed saving, selecting and preserving seeds from their best-performing crops for future planting.
- **Community Seed Banks**: Initiatives establishing community seed banks, like the one in Odisha, empower farmers to access and exchange diverse seed varieties.

4. Promotion of Underutilized Crops

- **Millets and Indigenous Grains**: Efforts to promote and cultivate millets and indigenous grains, such as ragi and jowar, highlight their nutritional value and resilience to adverse conditions.
- **Slow Food Movement**: Advocates for biodiversity in agriculture, emphasizing the consumption of local, traditional, and sustainably produced foods.

5. Challenges in Seed Preservation

- **Commercialization and Hybridization**: Increased focus on high-yielding varieties and hybrids has marginalized indigenous seed varieties, risking their extinction.
- **Loss of Traditional Knowledge**: Rapid urbanization and changing agricultural practices contribute to the erosion of traditional seed-saving practices.

6. Governmental Support and Policies

- **National Seed Policy**: India's National Seed Policy aims to promote the development, production, and supply of quality seeds, including indigenous varieties.
- **Biodiversity Conservation Laws**: Legal frameworks like the Biological Diversity Act facilitate the conservation of biodiversity, including traditional seeds.

VIII. Challenges and Future Prospects

1. Land Degradation and Soil Health

- **Erosion and Degradation**: Increasing erosion, salinization, and depletion of soil fertility pose significant threats to agricultural productivity.
- **Need for Soil Rejuvenation**: Implementing regenerative agriculture practices to restore soil health and combat land degradation is crucial.

2. Economic Viability and Market Access

- **Cost of Transition**: For many farmers, the initial costs of transitioning to sustainable practices, certification expenses, and reduced yields during the transition period pose financial challenges.
- **Market Linkages**: Ensuring fair prices and reliable markets for organic and sustainably produced goods remains a hurdle.

3. Technology Integration and Education

- **Adoption of Technology**: Bridging the gap between traditional wisdom and modern agricultural technologies is essential for enhancing productivity while preserving sustainability.
- **Farmer Education**: Continuous education and training programs are necessary to equip farmers with the skills and knowledge to adopt and sustain sustainable practices.

4. Water Scarcity and Efficient Use:

- **Depleting Water Resources**: Escalating water scarcity demands efficient water management techniques and the adoption of drought-resistant crops.
- **Innovative Irrigation Methods**: Further development and dissemination of water-saving irrigation systems are pivotal.

5. Policy Implementation and Support:

- **Effective Implementation**: Bridging the gap between policies and on-ground implementation is crucial for successful adoption of sustainable farming practices.
- **Financial Support**: Ensuring adequate financial and infrastructural support from government schemes for farmers transitioning to sustainable practices.

6. Consumer Awareness and Demand

- **Educating Consumers**: Building awareness among consumers about the benefits of sustainable produce is essential to drive demand and support the market for such products.
- **Changing Consumption Patterns**: Encouraging shifts in consumer behavior towards supporting sustainable and locally produced food.

Conclusion

In India, the trajectory towards sustainable farming practices represents a transformative journey, amalgamating ancient wisdom with modern innovations to address pressing environmental, social, and economic challenges. The pursuit of sustainable agriculture is not merely a choice but a necessity, driven by the imperative to secure food production, preserve natural resources, and ensure the well-being of present and future generations. The chapters explored India's rich heritage of sustainable farming, showcasing ancient practices from the Indus Valley Civilization, the integration of Ayurvedic principles, the exponential growth of organic farming, and innovative water conservation techniques. As we conclude this exploration, the call to action resonates strongly—to uphold and expand sustainable farming practices, to bridge the gap between traditional wisdom and modern techniques, and to foster a shared responsibility in nurturing the earth for the well-being of all life forms. The journey towards sustainable farming in India is an ongoing endeavor, crucial for fostering resilience, ensuring food security, and leaving a legacy of stewardship for generations to come.

References

Kalu, B. A. & Fick, G. W. (2011). Quantifying morphological development of alfalfa for studies of herbage quality. *Crop Science, 21,* 267–271.

Kohel, R. J. (2013). Genetic nomenclature in cotton. *Journal of Heredity, 64,* 291–295.

Leonard, W. H., Love, R. M. & Heath, M. E. (2018). Crop terminology today. *Crop Science, 8,* 257–261.

Little, T. M. (2008). If Galileo published in HortScience. *HortScience 13,* 504–506.

Moore, K. J., Moser, L. E., Vogel, K. P., Waller, S. S., Johnson, B. E. & Pedersen, J. F. (2011). Describing and quantifying growth stages of perennial forage grasses. *Agronomy Journal, 83,* 1073–1077.

Nelson, L. A. & Rawlings, J. O. (2013). Ten common misuses of statistics in agronomic research and reporting. *Journal of Agronomic Education, 12,* 100–105.

Webb, E. C. (Ed.). (2022). Enzyme nomenclature, 1992: Recommendations of the Nomenclature Committee of the International Union of Biochemistry and Molecular Biology on the nomenclature and classification of enzymes. *Academic Press,*23-29.

2

From Field to Market: Strategic Approaches to Agricultural Marketing

Rajiv Nayan Das

MGN Fellow, IIM Bangalore, Karnataka

Abstract

With the rapid growing market and ever-changing technologies, agriculture is also changing. The expanding market space is demanding strategic approaches to agricultural marketing in order to achieve its full potential. The chapter provides a basic understanding of market, its dimensions and structure to provide an understanding of a general market. It highlights the peculiarities of Agricultural marketing, sighting how its marketing is more complex and necessary in present context. It concludes with few important concepts of marketing which could be applied into agricultural enterprises in order to enhance its efficiency and improve returns.

Keywords: *Market, Agricultural Marketing, Strategy, Market Dynamics*

Introduction

Agriculture came into existence around 12,000 years ago laying foundations for human civilization, helping people to live in a permanent settlement instead of a continuous nomadic lifestyle. The primitive form of farming was subsistence farming, where all the crops and livestock raised by the farmers was solely for the consumption of their family or community. People exchanged what they produced. The activity of marketing was just an activity of distribution. With development of civilization with social stratification, developed transportation and communication, the process of marketing became necessary and complex at the same time.

As per historians the earliest form of market came into existence during 1500 BCE in the Mesopotamian civilization when their societies started mass production of goods that required quality control. Agricultural commodities have been a major component in markets of every civilization all across the world.

This chapter discuss regarding the basics of Agricultural Markting, its need and functions regarding various marketing strategies for agricultural products and peculiarities of agriculture marketing.

Knowing the Market

A **market** is where parties can gather to facilitate the exchange of goods and services.

A Markets Place is physical in nature like Mandis or Haats while the term Market Space encompasses any form of market, be it physical or virtual like e-retailer, social media etc.

Marketing

- ❖ Marketing is about identifying the human and social needs and meeting them profitably.
- ❖ As per American Marketing Association "**Marketing** is defined as an organizational function and a set of processes for creating, communicating, and delivering value to customers and maintaining customer relationships in ways that benefit the organization and its stakeholders."

Dimensions of A Market

There are various dimensions of any specified market. These dimensions are:

1. Location
2. Area or coverage
3. Time span
4. Volume of transactions
5. Nature of transactions
6. Number of commodities
7. Degree of competition
8. Nature of commodities
9. Stage of marketing
10. Extent of public intervention
11. Type of population served
12. Accrual of marketing margins

Any individual market may be classified in a twelve-dimensional space.

Market Structure

It refers to the terms and characteristics of the market which affects the mode of operation and conduct of business firms in the market influencing nature of competition, pricing etc.

The structural characteristics of the market govern the behavior of the firms in planning strategies for their selling and buying operations.

Components of Market Structure

1. **Market Power Concentration**: The Market Power is determined by the number and size of firms existing in the market. The more a firm has control over buying and selling of the product, the more concentrated is its market power which allows them to control and restrict the transaction of product at fair and competitive prices. It determines the nature of competition in market and subsequently affects market conduct and performance.
2. **Degree of Product Differentiation:** One or more additional qualities of a product which differentiates it from its contemporaries determines the degree of product differentiation in a firm.

   Homogenous products have less price variation in market. Heterogenous products have more differentiation in terms of quality and experience in order to prove one superior than other which leads to higher price variation.

   For example, Tea is a more Homogenous product with limited price range while there are is a high degree of product differentiation in Coffee market.
3. **Entry Barriers/ Conditions:** Any kind of restriction/regulations by the Government or the existing firms of industry to start the business is called as an Entry Barrier. The barriers need not to be a legality issue always, it also may be cultural or financial in nature.

   For example, there is need of huge capital investments to enter into Aviation Industry which restricts the entry to only a certain class of businessmen.
4. **Flow of Market information:** Market information mainly consists of the price distribution of products and offer prices of different sellers in the market. It also tries to provide an estimate of market demand based on current situations and past year trends.

   A well-organized market intelligence information system helps all the buyers and sellers to freely interact with one another in arriving at prices and striking deals.
5. **Degree of Integration:** Integration in market refers to two or more operation in the supply chain of a product is controlled by one firm or multiple firms with similar marketing functions are controlled by a single entity.

An integrated market will be comparatively less fluctuating, compared to a market where there is no integration either among the firms or of their activities

The market structure, always have to keep on adjusting to the changing environment to satisfy the social goals. A static market structure soon becomes obsolete because of the changes in the physical, economic, institutional and technological factors. For a satisfactory market performance, the market structure should keep pace with the Production Pattern, Demand pattern, costs and patterns of marketing function and most importantly, technological changes in the industry.

Agricultural Marketing

As per The National Commission on Agriculture:

'**Agricultural marketing** is a process which starts with a decision to produce a saleable farm commodity and it involves all aspects of market structure of system, both functional and institutional, based on technical and economic considerations and includes pre and post- harvest operations, assembling, grading, storage, transportation and distribution.'

The Indian council of Agricultural Research defined involvement of three important functions, namely:

i. Assembling (concentration)

ii. Preparation for consumption (processing) and

iii. Distribution

Agricultural Marketing comprises of all activities involved in agriculture, from supply of farm inputs to movement of agricultural produce from the farms to the consumers. The role of marketing starts right from the time of decision what to produce, which variety to produce and how to prepare the product for marketing rather than limiting to when, where and whom to sell.

Major Actors of Agricultural Market

Any product has a supply chain, starting from its producer and ending at the end consumer. It is important to be aware of the motives of the major actors of supply chain to strategically operate in the market. The major actors of supply chain of any agricultural products are:

Producers: Farmers want to obtain the inputs at least cost possible and sell the output at earliest after their harvest. They want the maximum share of the consumer's rupee spent on their produce.

Consumers: A consumer in an agricultural market wants to obtain his/her food on demand at the lowest price possible. The food should be of their desired quality and available in their required quantity.

Middlemen/Traders: Middlemen are the necessary evil of the market system. Their objective is to purchase the agricultural produce at low price from farmers and sell it to consumers at a high price. They are usually involved in one or more important marketing functions like transportation, wholesale and retail sales, etc.

Government: As we can see, the objectives of the all three groups above, clashes with each other. The government takes care that all groups of market with its rules and regulations and beneficiary schemes in order to run a marketing system for overall benefit of society. The Government takes action to eliminate unnecessary middlemen and regulates hoarding of agricultural produce in order to give farmers their fair share while keeping the market prices low for consumers.

Need of Agricultural Marketing

With commercialization of Agriculture over ages, technological interventions and high **marketable surplus,** marketing has become a necessity in agriculture. Agricultural marketing includes Input as well as product marketing.

Input marketing deals with industries producing genetically modified seeds, fertilizers and pesticides, organic manures etc that are used by farmers for producing crops. It has gained importance in last 100 years with green revolution and commercial farming.

Output marketing refers to marketing of the crops produced by farmers. It has been happening since civilizations, but in today's scenario, with new technology, market intelligence, high-end weather forecast and online marketing opportunities, efficient marketing of agricultural products has become more challenging.

The marketing of any agricultural produce is challenging as compared to any other manufactured goods due to some peculiar factors. It is necessary to know these factors and understand how they influence the demand and supply of agricultural products in the market in order to understand the need of agricultural marketing:

1. **Perishability of the product:** As every farm product is perishable over time unlike manufactured goods, it sets a time period for marketing of the product. After harvest, it needs to be stored and transported in proper conditions to avoid decay of produce. Higher the perishability of the farm product, lower is the bargaining power of the farmers.
2. **Seasonality of Production:** Unlike manufactured goods, agricultural produce cannot be uniformly manufactured throughout the year. Every crop has a suitable season in which it is grown. Depending on their perishability, they are marketed just after harvest (vegetables) or throughout the year (pulses and cereals). Also due to lack of storage facilities, most farmers have to sell their products during harvest season at low prices. This causes significant fluctuation in prices of agricultural commodities throughout a year.
3. **Bulkiness of Products:** Farm products are bulky in nature which increases their storage and transportation cost. It also reduces the distance of market where a farmer can sell their product. Most of the farmers sell in local market or handover the produce to big traders at lower price to be sold at distant market.
4. **Variation in Quality of Products:** Due to different varieties and different raising conditions, there is a large variation in the quality of farm products. This makes the grading and standardization of the products difficult, which is not an issue in case of manufactured goods.
5. **Small scale and scattered production:** Majority of farmers in India are marginal in nature with a land holding of less than 1 hectare. They operate

independently cultivating the crop suitable to their knowledge and finances. This makes it very difficult to estimate the supply of crops in market.

6. **Processing:** Several crops like Paddy cannot be consumed without processing. Often the rice mill owners form a cartel which forces farmers to operate as per their conditions. These processing firms enjoy the advantage of oligopsony, duopsony or even monopsony at some markets.

Importance Of Agricultural Marketing

When a country shifts from traditional agriculture to Modern agriculture, a marketing problem arises because of the production surplus generated. An efficient agricultural marketing system plays the crucial role there, to reduce the post-harvest losses, market surplus produces efficiently and increase the share of a farmer in consumer's rupee. The term Modern agriculture can be also referred as Market oriented agriculture.

The importance of Agricultural Marketing in economic development of the country can be summarised with following points:

i. Optimization of Resource use and Output Management

ii. Increase in Farm Income by reducing middlemen and commissions

iii. Widening of Markets through better transportation and exports

iv. Growth of Agro-Based Industries

v. Price Signals: Helps farmers in planning their production in accordance with the needs of the economy

vi. Adoption and Spread of New Technology

vii. Employment to millions in allied activities like storage, processing, packaging and transporting etc.

viii. Addition to National income by adding value to products through marketing

ix. Increase standard of living through efficient marketing of food and agricultural products

x. Creation of Utility: Any product realises its utility only when it reaches the right place at right time in the form as required by the consumer. The process of marketing helps a product to realise or create its utility. There are four types of utility which can be created by marketing:

   a) Form Utility: It means changing the form of the harvested product by processing it into a consumable finished form. For Example, Paddy to Rice, Cotton to thread, Wheat grains to flour, etc.

   b) Place Utility: The price of a product is more at the place of need than the place where it is harvested. The transportation function helps to add this place utility to the products by delivering them at the place of needs.

For example: The price of Apple is Shimla is much less than its price in Mumbai

c) Time Utility: The storage function adds time utility to the products by making them available till the time they are needed. For Example: Price of tomato drastically reduce during its harvest season like February but a high demand arises during the months of June-July.

d) Possession Utility: Through the marketing functions the products are transferred to persons having higher utility from person having lower utility. For example, A tractor has higher utility with a farmer than a showroom owner.

Significant Agricultural Marketing Functions

Marketing function are activities aimed at adding values to a product. It may be any one or combination of three dimensions viz. time, space and form.

As we saw how processing, transportation and storage functions add several utilities to the agricultural products above, here we will discuss some other significant marketing functions that add utility to agricultural products.

Procurement & Assembling: It is the process of collecting several similar or different, related or unrelated products and assembling it a common platform to make it available easily to consumers.

For examples, the supermarket collects vegetables from different farmers to sell at one place.

Packaging: Packaging means putting the goods on the market in the size and pack which are convenient for the buyers. It is one of the most important aspects of agricultural marketing. Every product requires a different packaging and storage conditions in order to obtain maximum shelf life.

Besides protecting the goods from damage and adulteration, packaging is also necessary for branding and labelling of commodities.

Grading & Standardization:

Standardization refers to determination of standards to be established for different commodities on the basis of characteristics such as size, colour, texture, weight, ripeness, sweetness, amount of foreign matter etc. It makes clear quality specification of different grades so that each grade of product could be easily differentiated by the buyers and sellers.

Grading means sorting of varying standard or quality of produce into different categories as per the pre-determined quality specifications. It is a sub function of standardization.

Grading helps in providing a uniform quality standards knowledge base for buyers and sellers on whose basis prices can be decided and trading could be easily done without mandatory physical verification of quality. It helps the producers to find their target customer easily. It also increases return of the farmers and makes the product insurable.

In India, under The Agricultural Produce (Grading and Marking) Act, 1937 there are 153 commodities including food grains, oilseeds, fruits & vegetables, dairy, coffee, tobacco, edible oils, cotton, sun hemp, edible nuts, jaggery, lac, spices and condiments, honey, besan, suji & Maida etc. for which the government has laid out grade standards. The Agricultural Marketing Advisor (AMA) to Govt. of India is the authority to implement the provisions of the act and suggest suitable modifications.

Market Information

Market information is a communication or reception of a news or intelligence information which may affect the busing and selling of goods and service in a market. It is based on facts, estimates, opinions, trends etc.

Market information is like lifeblood of a market. Correct market information helps to take decision regarding when and where to market how much products. It helps the government to make policies for market regulation, buffer stocking, import-export and administered prices.

Financing

Finance is a necessity of all the components of agricultural market. The producers need finance during cropping season for purchase of seeds and fertilizers. The seller needs finance during harvest season to procure crops and sell in market. The middle men need finance to carry out several functions like storage, processing, packaging, transportation etc. In the words of Pyle: "Money or credit is the lubricant that facilitates the marketing machine."

In India, National Bank for Agriculture and Rural Development (NABARD) was set up in 1984 as an apex organization in the sphere of agricultural and rural finance. It provides refinancing support to financial institutions for financing wide range of activities pertaining to agriculture and rural development, starting from farm loan to development of cold storages and warehouses, processing and cooperative marketing, etc.

Strategies For Efficient Agricultural Marketing

Strategy can be defined as a plan or set of actions dedicated to achieve a long-term goal. In order to avoid post-harvest losses and gain maximum share in a consumer's rupee, the farmers/producers need to be aware of some concepts of marketing which would help them to make strategies. An ideal marketing strategy begins from selection of crop and ends with delivering the produce to the target consumer.

Here are few marketing important concepts:

1. Marketing Mix: McCarthy classified the concept of marketing Mix into four broad groups referred as 4 Ps of Marketing. The 4Ps in order are **Product, Price, Place and Promotion.**

Later Robert Lauterborn suggested that the 4Ps of a seller should serve the **4Cs of a customer** as in a Product should provide **Customer Solution**

Price should represent **Customer cost**

Place should provide **Convenience** to customer and

Promotion should enable a 2-way **Communication**

So, while producing a crop the farmer should take care that the consumer has demand for the product, the price range which the customer is willing to pay for it, where the consumer locates (rural or urban) and does the consumer have knowledge regarding the sale of the product.

2. SWOT Analysis: SWOT stands for the **Strength, Weakness, Opportunity** and **Threats.** This analysis encompasses the possible effect that internal and external environment may have on a business which is necessary for strategic planning.

While the Strength and Weakness are part of the internal environmental factors (micro environment), the opportunities and threats come from the external environment of an enterprise. While the internal factors can be controlled by an organization, the knowledge of external factors would help the enterprise to be prepared take the blow or get benefited from an opportunity.

An example of SWOT analysis of a Potato crop is presented below in table 1.

Table 1

I N T E R N A L	Strength	Opportunity	E X T E R N A L
	Soil condition Irrigation facility Storage facility	High price in neighbouring state Value Addition	
	Weakness	Threats	
	Poor Drainage Labour cost for harvest Transportation	Splash Rain/storm Insect/Pest attack Quarantine restrictions for disease	

The Macro environment of an enterprise deals with these factors, which can be categorised into six categories. It is referred as **PESTEL** in short, which stands for factors like:

Political: Example: Political ideologies leading to ban on non-vegetarian foods

Economic: Example: Inflation & Unemployment reducing demand

Social: Example: Attitude towards work, Social acceptance of a product

Technological: Example: Power tiller reducing demand of tractors

Environmental: Example: Climate change, Uneven rainfall

Legal: Example: Food Certification and quality control laws, Pesticide residue limits

3. Post Harvest Treatments

As per NABCONS Study 2022, the post-harvest loss in pulses and cereals in 5-6% while in case of fruits and vegetables it ranges around 10-15% in India. Proper Post harvest practices could increase the shelf life of products and provide higher return to the farmers.

Post harvest handling mostly includes activities like cleaning, sorting and packaging which helps in grading and storage of product and thus helps in providing higher returns.

Example: Proper drying and storage of maize to protect it from mold, pests and moisture.

4. Cluster approach to farming

Majority of farmers are marginal in India with land holdings of less tant 1 Ha. The individual operation in small land holdings increases the cost of input, cultivation, harvesting and marketing for a farmer. Cluster approach is an efficient strategy for utilising economies of scale to develop self-sufficient units of production. It allows for combining efforts, making use of synergies and pooling resources to increase competitive advantage while sharing market risks.

For farm related activities, producer groups could be formed at initial stage with 10-15 farmers per group to carry out farming with a cluster approach. To increase the scale several such producer groups come together to form a Farmer Producer Company (**FPC**) or Farmer Producer Organization (**FPO**) registered under Indian Companies act 1956 or Cooperative Societies Act, 1962 respectively. Its advantages are listed below:

i. Larger working capital helps in improving farm mechanization

ii. Wholesale/Bulk purchase of seeds and fertilizers reduces individual cost of farmers spent on inputs

iii. Quality control would be easier and could be easily monitored

iv. Shared market risks and cost of transportation

v. Higher bargaining power

5. Online Marketing/ e-NAM

With technology advancements, the market has gone online. Use of platforms like National Agriculture Market (eNAM) and ITC e-Choupal could help the farmers to sell their produce at better price with much ease. There are various private platforms like India Mart and shopping apps which connects buyers and sellers of Agri-produce all over the county and world. The online platform could also be used to gather market information and strategize sale accordingly.

Conclusion

With commercialization of agriculture, marketing has become an integral part of agriculture. With technological advancements and internet, the producers need to adapt and evolve in the changing market in order to stay significant and gain from agri-business. The basic knowledge of market, its operation, structure, functions and various concepts will provide a base to design strategies for agri-business and marketing.

Puzzle to Solve

A list of marketing functions if provided in List 1. You are supposed to allocate each function to box A, B, C or D as per the utility they add to a product. Note that, one function may add more than one utility to a product.

<table>
<tr><th>List – 1- Marketing Functions</th><th>A- Form Utility</th><th>B- Place Utility</th></tr>
<tr><td rowspan="3">Assembling and Procurement
Processing
Packaging
Transportation
Grading & Standardization
Storage
Determining Need
Financing
Market News
Market Intelligence
Buying and selling
Risk Bearing</td><td>Packaging</td><td>T..........</td></tr>
<tr><th>C- Time Utility</th><th>D- Possession Utility</th></tr>
<tr><td>Storage</td><td>M............</td></tr>
</table>

References

Acharya, S.S. (2004). *Agricultural marketing in India.* Oxford and IBH publishing.

Babatunde, B. O., & Adebisi, A. O. (2012). Strategic Environmental Scanning and Organization Performance in a Competitive Business Environment. *Economic Insights-Trends & Challenges, 64*(1).

Gamble, J., Gilmore, A., McCartan-Quinn, D., & Durkan, P. (2011). The Marketing concept in the 21st century: A review of how Marketing has been defined since the 1960s. *The marketing review, 11*(3), 227-248.

Kamien, M. I., & Schwartz, N. L. (1975). Market structure and innovation: A survey. *Journal of economic literature, 13*(1), 1-37.

Rao, S & Reddy, B. LECTURE NOTES Course No. AECO 341 Agricultural Marketing.

Wani, T. (2013). From 4Ps to SAVE: A theoretical analysis of various marketing mix models. *Business Sciences International Research Journal, 1*(1).

3

Cultivating the Future Empowering Youth in Agriculture

Sidharth Dash

Assistant Manager (Livelihood), CBSAE Development. Project, OUAT Bhubaneswar, Odisha, India

Abstract

With the global population burgeoning, the agricultural landscape faces unprecedented challenges—demand for increased food production, climate change, and the aging farming population. Empowering youth emerges as a critical solution to these challenges, offering a pathway to innovation, resilience, and sustainability. This chapter delves into the pivotal role of youth empowerment in agriculture for sustainable development. Highlighting the challenges hindering youth engagement, it proposes solutions centered on education reform, technological integration, and supportive policies. Success stories and initiatives from various regions showcase effective approaches, emphasizing mentorship, digital platforms, and entrepreneurship to attract and develop youth in agriculture. It stresses the importance of partnerships among governments, NGOs, and private sectors, advocating for collaborative efforts to provide comprehensive support and opportunities. By investing in the next generation of agricultural leaders, this chapter emphasizes the potential for a thriving, innovative, and resilient agricultural sector capable of meeting the demands of a rapidly changing world.

Keywords: *Youth Empowerment, Agriculture, Sustainability, Innovation, Engagement*

Introduction

The agricultural sector stands at a crossroads, facing the dual challenge of meeting the escalating global demand for food while grappling with the impact of climate change and an aging farming population. In this context, the empowerment of youth emerges as a beacon of hope, holding the key to transforming agriculture into a dynamic, sustainable, and innovative sector. This chapter embarks on a journey to explore the pivotal role of empowering youth in agriculture, underscoring its significance not only on a global scale but also within the vibrant context of India, notably in the state of Odisha.

India, a country with a rich agricultural heritage, stands as a microcosm of both the challenges and opportunities present in the agricultural landscape. The nation grapples with the pressing need to enhance agricultural productivity while ensuring environmental sustainability. Within this expansive canvas, the state of Odisha emerges as a focal point due to its unique blend of traditional agricultural practices, diverse ecosystems, and a burgeoning youth population eager to contribute to the sector's evolution. Odisha's agricultural landscape presents a tapestry of challenges, including limited access to modern agricultural practices, climatic uncertainties, and the need for sustainable resource management. However, amid these challenges lies immense potential, especially within its youth demographic. The state's youth, armed with ambition, creativity, and a desire for change, stand poised to revolutionize Odisha's agricultural paradigm.

Moreover, India's national initiatives, such as the "Atmanirbhar Bharat" (Self-reliant India) campaign and various agricultural reforms, provide a backdrop for exploring how youth empowerment aligns with these ambitious goals. By fostering an environment that nurtures the entrepreneurial spirit of its youth and integrates technological advancements, India, with Odisha at its helm, can pave the way for a thriving, resilient, and sustainable agricultural future.Within this intricate interplay of challenges, opportunities, and aspirations, the chapter navigates the multifaceted landscape of youth empowerment in agriculture, underscoring its critical importance for India's agricultural resurgence, with Odisha serving as a vibrant microcosm reflecting the broader national context.Top of FormTop of Form

I. Understanding the Importance of Engaging Youth in Agriculture

i. The Evolution of Agriculture

Tracing Historical Significance

Agriculture has been fundamental to human civilization. This section would delve into the origins of agriculture, showcasing its pivotal role in the development of societies. Starting from hunter-gatherer practices to the Neolithic revolution, it demonstrates how cultivation of crops and domestication of animals revolutionized human settlements.

- **Historical Significance:** Highlighting milestones such as the transition from nomadic lifestyles to settled communities, the invention of tools, and the growth of early agricultural practices.
- **Cultural Impact:** Discussing how agriculture shaped cultural practices, social structures, and economies of ancient civilizations, emphasizing its centrality in human history.

Transformation of Agriculture and Its Relevance Today

This part bridges the historical evolution to the contemporary landscape, showing the evolution of agriculture through various revolutions - industrial, green, and technological.

- **Industrial Revolution:** Discussing how mechanization and mass production transformed farming methods and increased productivity.
- **Green Revolution:** Exploring the mid-20th-century advancements in plant breeding, chemical fertilizers, and pesticides, revolutionizing crop yields.
- **Technological Advancements:** Highlighting the modern era of precision agriculture, genetic engineering, IoT, and AI, showcasing their impact on efficiency, sustainability, and global food security.

Relevance Today

Tying historical evolution to the current context, emphasizing the relevance of understanding past transformations for addressing present challenges and opportunities.

- **Modern Agricultural Landscape:** Detailing the contemporary state of agriculture, discussing issues like climate change, food security, and sustainability.
- **Lessons from History:** Extracting lessons from the past to inform future agricultural practices, policies, and the importance of youth involvement in shaping agriculture's future trajectory.

By tracing this evolution, this section aims to contextualize the significance of agriculture in human development while laying the groundwork for why involving youth in this sector is crucial for its continued progress and sustainability.

ii. Top of Form

Challenges Faced by the Agricultural Sector

Aging Farmer Population

- **Description:** The current agricultural workforce is aging, with fewer young individuals entering the sector.
- **Impact:** This trend raises concerns about a potential shortage of skilled labor and knowledge transfer, posing a threat to the sustainability of agriculture.

Climate Change and Environmental Pressures

- **Description:** Agriculture is highly susceptible to climate change impacts, including unpredictable weather patterns, soil degradation, and water scarcity.
- **Impact:** These environmental challenges threaten crop yields, livestock health, and overall food production, requiring innovative solutions to ensure sustainability.

Access to Markets and Global Competition

- **Description:** Farmers often struggle to access markets due to limited resources or lack of infrastructure, while facing competition from global markets.
- **Impact:** Limited market access affects profitability, especially for small-scale farmers, hindering their economic growth and stability.

Technological and Educational Gaps

- **Description:** Disparities in technological adoption and access to education hinder productivity and innovation in many agricultural regions.
- **Impact:** Without adequate technological advancements and educational resources, farms struggle to remain competitive and sustainable.

II. Empowering Youth Through Education and Awareness

i. Top of Form

Role of Educational Programs in Agricultural Empowerment

Formal Education Integration

- **Curriculum Development:** Encouraging inclusion of agricultural subjects in formal education systems at primary, secondary, and higher education levels.
- **Agricultural Schools/Colleges:** Establishing specialized institutions focusing on agricultural sciences, offering comprehensive education and practical training.

Vocational and Technical Training

- **Skill Development:** Providing vocational courses, workshops, and training programs that equip youth with hands-on agricultural skills.
- **Internships and Practical Exposure:** Offering opportunities for real-world experience through internships at farms, agribusinesses, and research institutes.

ii. Promoting Agricultural Knowledge Among Young Individuals

Outreach Programs and Workshops

- **Community Engagement:** Conducting workshops, seminars, and outreach programs in rural and urban areas to introduce youth to agricultural concepts and practices.
- **Demonstration Farms:** Establishing farms or demonstration plots to showcase modern and sustainable agricultural techniques to young individuals.

Digital Learning Platforms

- **Online Courses and Resources:** Creating digital platforms offering courses, webinars, and educational resources accessible to youth, promoting self-learning.
- **Mobile Applications:** Developing mobile apps providing information on farming techniques, market trends, weather forecasts, and agricultural best practices.

iii. Encouraging Interdisciplinary Learning:

Cross-Disciplinary Approach

- **Integration with Other Fields:** Highlighting the interdisciplinary nature of agriculture by connecting it with subjects like biology, environmental science, economics, and technology.
- **Entrepreneurship Education:** Offering courses that combine agricultural knowledge with entrepreneurship skills to inspire innovative thinking.

Research and Innovation Hubs

- **Innovation Centers:** Establishing research hubs and innovation centers within educational institutions, fostering creativity and problem-solving in agricultural practices.
- **Student-led Projects:** Encouraging students to initiate and lead research projects addressing agricultural challenges, promoting critical thinking and innovation.

Partnerships and Collaboration

Public-Private Partnerships

- **Industry Collaboration:** Partnering with agricultural businesses, NGOs, and governmental bodies to provide mentorship, funding, and internship opportunities.
- **Alumni Networks:** Leveraging alumni networks to create mentorship programs, connecting experienced professionals with aspiring young farmers.

Evaluation and Improvement

Continuous Assessment and Feedback

- **Monitoring and Evaluation:** Regularly assessing the effectiveness of educational programs and modifying approaches based on feedback and evolving industry needs.
- **Long-term Impact Assessment:** Evaluating the long-term impact of educational initiatives on youth participation in agriculture and food security.

By fostering a comprehensive educational environment that encompasses formal education, vocational training, digital learning, interdisciplinary approaches, and collaborative efforts, institutions can effectively empower youth with the necessary knowledge and skills to thrive in the agricultural sector.

iv. Top of Form

Impact of Technology in Agriculture

Precision Farming Techniques

- **IoT and Sensors:** Implementing IoT devices and sensors for data collection on soil moisture, temperature, and crop health, enabling precise resource allocation.
- **GIS and GPS:** Using Geographic Information Systems (GIS) and Global Positioning Systems (GPS) for accurate mapping, planning, and monitoring of agricultural activities.

Automation and Robotics

- **Smart Machinery:** Deploying automated machinery for planting, harvesting, and irrigation, reducing labor and enhancing efficiency.
- **Drones and UAVs:** Utilizing drones for aerial monitoring, crop health assessment, and spraying, improving crop management.

Data-Driven Decision Making

- **Big Data Analytics:** Analyzing large volumes of agricultural data to optimize crop planning, predict market trends, and mitigate risks.
- **AI and Machine Learning:** Employing AI algorithms for predictive analysis, disease detection, and yield optimization.

Role of Digital Literacy in Farming

Access to Information and Resources

- **Digital Tools and Platforms:** Training farmers in using digital platforms for market information, weather forecasts, and agricultural best practices.
- **Online Resources:** Educating farmers on accessing online databases, research papers, and forums for continual learning.

Adoption of Technology

- **Capacity Building:** Providing training programs to enhance farmers' understanding and proficiency in using technology.
- **Troubleshooting and Maintenance:** Teaching farmers to troubleshoot basic technical issues and perform maintenance of digital tools.

Improving Efficiency and Sustainability

- **Resource Optimization:** Demonstrating how digital tools help in optimizing water usage, fertilizer application, and pest control, leading to sustainable practices.

- **Cost Reduction:** Highlighting how technology adoption can reduce operational costs and increase overall farm profitability.

III. Fostering Entrepreneurship and Innovation

i. Cultivating an Entrepreneurial Mindset

Embracing Risk-Taking and Creativity

- **Risk-Tolerance:** Encouraging a willingness to take calculated risks, experiment with new ideas, and learn from failures.
- **Creative Problem-Solving:** Stimulating creativity to identify innovative solutions for agricultural challenges.

Vision and Opportunity Recognition

- **Future-oriented Thinking:** Cultivating a forward-looking approach that identifies emerging trends, market gaps, and opportunities.
- **Adaptability:** Being open to adapt and pivot strategies in response to changing market demands or environmental factors.

Encouraging Innovation in Farming Practices

Experimentation and Adaptation

- **Trial and Error:** Encouraging experimentation with new techniques, technologies, and farming methods.
- **Adopting Sustainable Practices:** Promoting environmentally conscious approaches while ensuring profitability.

Value-Added Agriculture

- **Product Diversification:** Encouraging the development of value-added products like organic produce, specialty crops, or artisanal goods.
- **Brand Building:** Emphasizing the importance of branding, marketing, and creating a unique selling proposition for farm products.

ii. Strategies to Promote Entrepreneurship Among Young Farmers

Education and Training Programs

- **Entrepreneurship Courses:** Integrating entrepreneurship education into agricultural programs, teaching business skills alongside technical knowledge.
- **Incubator Programs:** Offering incubation and startup support programs specifically tailored for young agricultural entrepreneurs.

Access to Resources and Funding

- **Financial Support:** Providing access to grants, loans, or venture capital specifically for young farmers and agripreneurs.

- **Access to Land and Infrastructure:** Facilitating access to land, equipment, and infrastructure necessary for starting and scaling up agricultural businesses.

Mentorship and Networking

Mentorship Programs

- **Experienced Guidance:** Pairing young farmers with experienced mentors who provide advice, guidance, and industry insights.
- **Networking Opportunities:** Creating platforms for networking with peers, industry experts, and potential partners or investors.

Collaboration and Knowledge Sharing

- **Community Engagement:** Encouraging collaboration within agricultural communities, sharing experiences, and lessons learned.
- **Industry Events and Forums:** Participating in industry events, workshops, and forums to gain exposure and network with other entrepreneurs.

Long-Term Impact and Sustainability

Sustainable Business Models

- **Social and Environmental Responsibility:** Encouraging the development of businesses that prioritize sustainability, social impact, and ethical practices.
- **Resilience and Growth:** Building businesses that are resilient to market fluctuations and capable of adapting to changing circumstances.

Advocacy and Policy Influence

- **Policy Advocacy:** Engaging in policy discussions to advocate for supportive regulations, incentives, and programs for young agricultural entrepreneurs.
- **Industry Representation:** Fostering a strong voice within the agricultural industry, influencing decisions and shaping its future.

By instilling an entrepreneurial mindset and providing the necessary support and resources, young farmers can be empowered to innovate, create value, and contribute to the sustainable growth and transformation of the agricultural sector.

iii. Supporting Youth-Led Agricultural Startups

Funding Mechanisms

- **Grants and Subsidies:** Providing financial support through government grants, subsidies, or specific funding programs targeting young entrepreneurs in agriculture.
- **Venture Capital and Angel Investors:** Facilitating access to investment networks focused on agricultural innovation and youth-led startups.

Incubator and Accelerator Programs

- **Startup Incubation:** Establishing incubators tailored to agricultural startups, offering mentorship, resources, and guidance for business development.
- **Accelerator Programs:** Providing intensive programs that fast-track the growth of promising agricultural startups through mentorship and networking opportunities.

Public-Private Partnerships

- **Industry Collaborations:** Partnering with agricultural businesses, corporations, or industry associations to provide mentorship, resources, and market access for startups.
- **Government Initiatives:** Collaborating with government bodies to create policies and programs that foster a conducive environment for youth-led agricultural initiatives.

IV. Overcoming Barriers and Addressing Challenges

i. Access to Resources

Land Access Challenges

- **Land Availability:** Discussing the scarcity of available land for young farmers due to high costs or limited availability.
- **Land Tenure Issues:** Addressing challenges related to land tenure security and access to agricultural land for lease or purchase.

Capital and Financial Constraints

- **Limited Funding:** Exploring the difficulties young farmers face in accessing loans, grants, or investment capital for starting or scaling up agricultural ventures.
- **High Input Costs:** Discussing challenges related to the affordability of agricultural inputs, machinery, and infrastructure.

Policy and Advocacy

Land Policies and Regulations

- **Land Reforms:** Advocating for policies that facilitate land access for young farmers through land redistribution, leasing schemes, or land banking initiatives.
- **Zoning and Land Use Planning:** Highlighting the importance of zoning policies that promote agricultural land use and protect agricultural spaces.

Financial Support and Incentives

- **Subsidies and Grants:** Advocating for government support programs offering subsidies, grants, or favorable loans for youth-led agricultural initiatives.

- **Tax Incentives:** Encouraging tax breaks or incentives for young farmers to stimulate investment and business growth.

Mentorship and Support Networks

Lack of Guidance and Experience

- **Mentorship Gap:** Discussing the absence of mentorship opportunities and the need for experienced guidance for young farmers.
- **Limited Networks:** Addressing challenges in building supportive networks and communities for mentorship and knowledge-sharing.

Importance of Mentorship Programs

- **Establishing Mentorship Programs:** Advocating for the creation of formal mentorship programs that pair experienced farmers with young individuals.
- **Training and Guidance:** Providing training on effective mentorship techniques and the importance of ongoing support.

Networking and Community Building

- **Community Support:** Emphasizing the role of community-based networks in providing support, information, and opportunities for collaboration among young farmers.
- **Online Platforms:** Promoting digital platforms or forums where young farmers can connect, share experiences, and access resources.

Collaboration for Change

Stakeholder Engagement

- **Government-Community Partnerships:** Encouraging collaboration between government bodies, NGOs, and local communities to address resource access issues.
- **Private Sector Engagement:** Involving private sector entities in mentorship programs and resource provision for young farmers.

Policy Advocacy Platforms

- **Youth Representation:** Encouraging youth involvement in policy discussions, ensuring their voices are heard in decision-making processes.
- **Awareness Campaigns:** Using advocacy campaigns to raise awareness about the challenges faced by young farmers and advocating for supportive policies.

Long-Term Sustainability and Impact

Continuity and Evaluation

- **Sustainability of Support Programs:** Advocating for long-term support programs that provide continuous assistance to young farmers beyond initial stages.

- **Impact Assessment:** Evaluating the effectiveness of support mechanisms and policy changes, adjusting strategies based on feedback and results.

Knowledge Sharing and Best Practices

- **Documentation and Case Studies:** Sharing success stories and best practices to inspire and guide other young farmers facing similar challenges.
- **Training and Capacity Building:** Continually providing training and capacity-building programs to empower young farmers with necessary skills.

By addressing barriers related to resources, advocating for supportive policies, and fostering mentorship and support networks, the agricultural sector can create an enabling environment for young farmers, encouraging their active participation and long-term success in agriculture.

Long-Term Sustainability Strategies

Education and Skill Development

- **Continual Learning:** Encouraging lifelong learning through ongoing education programs, workshops, and skill development initiatives.
- **Youth Engagement:** Involving young farmers in decision-making processes, ensuring their voices are heard in shaping agricultural policies.

Entrepreneurial Support

- **Business Incubation:** Establishing long-term incubator programs that provide ongoing mentorship and resources for young agricultural entrepreneurs.
- **Financial Sustainability:** Promoting financial literacy and management skills to ensure the financial sustainability of youth-led agricultural initiatives.

V. Success Stories and Inspirational Case Studies

i. Profiles of Young Farmers

Innovative Agricultural Entrepreneurs

- **Tech-Driven Farming:** Highlighting young farmers utilizing technology for precision farming, such as IoT, drones, or AI, to boost productivity.
- **Value-Added Products:** Showcasing individuals involved in producing value-added goods, such as organic foods, specialty crops, or unique products.

Sustainable Agriculture Advocates

- **Environmental Stewards:** Profiles of young farmers practicing regenerative agriculture, focusing on soil health, biodiversity, and conservation.
- **Community Engagement:** Stories of individuals fostering community-supported agriculture or engaging in local food movements.

Community Initiatives

Urban Farming and Community Gardens

- **Urban Agriculture Projects:** Showcasing young farmers leading initiatives in urban settings, utilizing small spaces for food production and education.
- **School and Youth Programs:** Highlighting projects involving schools or youth groups promoting agricultural learning and community engagement.

Farmer Cooperatives and Collective Efforts

- **Collective Enterprises:** Stories of young farmers coming together to form cooperatives, sharing resources, and improving market access.
- **Collaborative Projects:** Profiles of youth-led projects aimed at addressing local agricultural challenges through collaboration and collective action.

ii. Lessons Learned and Insights

Entrepreneurial Skills and Innovation

- **Risk-Taking and Adaptability:** Extracting lessons on embracing risks and adapting to market changes from successful entrepreneurial ventures.
- **Innovation and Technology Adoption:** Insights into the benefits of adopting technology and innovative farming methods for efficiency and growth.

Community Engagement and Impact

- **Building Support Networks:** Lessons on the importance of community engagement, mentorship, and collaboration for success in agriculture.
- **Sustainability Practices:** Insights into the impact of sustainable farming practices on both the environment and long-term business viability.

Reference

Desai, P. M. (2023). AI Integration in Indian Agricultural Extension. In S. Gupta & R. Jain (Eds.), *Innovative AI Solutions for Indian Farming*, pp. 123-140.

Gupta, M. (2023). Economic Viability of Agricultural Tech in India. In R. Kumar & S. Sharma (Eds.), *Economic Impacts of Farming Tech in India*, pp. 175-190.

Joshi, H. R. (2023). Data Privacy and Security in Indian Agricultural Tech. In M. Khanna & R. Agarwal (Eds.), *Secure Digital Agriculture in India* ,pp. 89-104.

Kapoor, S. R. & Reddy, V. (2023). Internet of Things (IoT) Revolutionizing Agriculture in India. In N. Verma & M. Kumar (Eds.), *Smart Farming for India's Future*, pp. 89-104.

Khan, A. (2023). Training and Capacity Building for Indian Farmers. In S. Bhat & M. Yadav (Eds.), *Empowering Indian Farmers through Technology Training*, pp. 145-160.

Mehta, N. R. (2023). Challenges and Opportunities in Indian Agricultural Tech. In A. Mishra & P. Sharma (Eds.), *Digital Revolution in Indian Agriculture*, pp. 55-70.

Patel, K. S. (2023). IoT Empowering Farmers in India. In B. Chauhan & A. Singh (Eds.), *IoT Applications in Indian Agriculture*, pp. 175-190.

Reddy, A. S. (2023). Sustainable Agriculture and Ethics in India. In P. Choudhury & S. Malhotra (Eds.), *Sustainable Farming Practices and Ethical Considerations in India*, pp. 215-230.

4

Revitalizing India's Ecosystem The Promise of Regenerative Agriculture

Sayan Sagnika Mohapatra

Odisha University of Agriculture & Technology, Bhubaneswar, Odisha, India

Abstract

The interplay between ecosystems and agriculture forms the bedrock of our sustenance. Ecosystems provide the fertile ground, the clean water, and the biodiversity necessary for agricultural productivity. Agriculture, in turn, impacts ecosystems - shaping landscapes, influencing biodiversity, and affecting natural resources. Balancing this relationship is crucial for sustainable food production and the preservation of Earth's natural balance. This chapter explores the transformative potential of regenerative agriculture within the intricate tapestry of India's farming milieu. It delves into the principles, challenges, and opportunities surrounding this holistic approach to farming, offering insights into its impact on ecosystems, farmer livelihoods, and food security. From success stories across diverse regions to the hurdles hindering widespread adoption, this exploration unveils the intricate balance between tradition and innovation. Emphasizing the need for policy reforms, education, technological integration, and community engagement, it outlines a roadmap for the future. The chapter underscores the significance of regenerative agriculture in restoring soil health, preserving biodiversity, and building resilience against climate change. It envisions a future where collaborative efforts and a cultural shift towards sustainable practices nurture a thriving agricultural landscape for India, ensuring a legacy of abundance and harmony with nature.

Keywords: *Regenerative Agriculture, Ecosystems, Sustainability, Biodiversity, Resilience*

Introduction

In the verdant landscapes and bustling fields of India, the heartbeat of a nation pulses through its agriculture. For millennia, farming has been not just a livelihood but an intrinsic part of the cultural fabric, shaping traditions, festivals, and the very essence of community life. Yet, the modern agricultural practices, driven by the pursuit of higher yields, have strained the very soil that nurtured this civilization for centuries. In this crucible of tradition and progress, a beacon of hope emerges - regenerative agriculture - offering a path to restore, revitalize, and safeguard India's precious ecosystems.

India, a land of diverse climates, terrains, and agricultural practices, faces a confluence of challenges in its farming landscape. The consequences of intensive chemical use, excessive tilling, and mono-cropping have left scars on the soil, depleting its fertility and compromising long-term sustainability. Climate change further amplifies these woes, introducing unpredictability in weather patterns, exacerbating water scarcity, and disrupting age-old farming calendars. For the millions of smallholder farmers, the backbone of India's agrarian economy, these challenges manifest as barriers to securing a stable livelihood and ensuring food security.

Amidst this landscape of trials and tribulations, regenerative agriculture emerges as a transformative paradigm. It transcends the boundaries of conventional sustainable farming practices by aiming not just to sustain but to regenerate ecosystems. At its core lies a profound philosophy, one that acknowledges the interconnectedness between the health of the land, biodiversity, and human well-being. Regenerative agriculture beckons farmers to embrace practices that mimic nature's wisdom, fostering resilience, and restoring vitality to the soil.

The allure of regenerative agriculture lies not just in its ethos but in its practicality. Its techniques, from minimal tillage and diverse crop rotations to the incorporation of cover crops and agroforestry, promise not only increased agricultural productivity but also the restoration of soil health and the preservation of precious water resources. This approach stands as a testament to the synergy between traditional wisdom and modern scientific advancements, harmonizing age-old indigenous practices with innovative technologies.

This journey toward regenerative agriculture in India is not solitary but collective—a collaboration between farmers, researchers, policymakers, and conscientious consumers. It necessitates a shift in mindset, an embrace of holistic and sustainable farming practices that respect the rhythms of nature. This book chapter embarks on an explorative odyssey, delving into the landscape of regenerative agriculture in India, unearthing success stories, addressing challenges, and illuminating a path toward a more resilient and thriving agricultural future.

Understanding Regenerative Agriculture

Regenerative agriculture, amidst the backdrop of environmental degradation and agricultural challenges, represents a paradigm shift in farming practices worldwide. At its essence, this approach isn't merely about sustaining agricultural production but rather about revitalizing ecosystems, nurturing soil health, and fostering resilience against the impacts of climate change. Understanding regenerative agriculture requires a deep dive into its principles, methodologies, and the transformative potential it holds for India's agricultural landscape.

At the heart of regenerative agriculture lies a profound respect for nature's intricate balance. It encompasses a holistic approach that integrates traditional wisdom with cutting-edge scientific knowledge. The fundamental principles revolve around fostering biodiversity, enhancing soil health, improving water retention, and sequestering carbon. By drawing inspiration from natural ecosystems, regenerative agriculture endeavors to emulate their resilience and efficiency.

Key practices define the essence of regenerative agriculture. Minimal tillage stands as a cornerstone, minimizing soil disturbance to preserve its structure and beneficial microorganisms. Crop rotation and diversification break the cycle of pests and diseases while enhancing soil fertility. Cover cropping shields the soil, curtails erosion, and replenishes nutrients. Agroforestry interweaves trees and crops, fostering biodiversity and enhancing ecosystem services.

In India, a country rich in agricultural heritage, the adoption of regenerative practices gains significance in mitigating the challenges faced by farmers. Historically, Indian agriculture thrived on sustainable principles, deeply rooted in indigenous knowledge. Regenerative agriculture builds upon this foundation, offering a contemporary framework that amalgamates age-old practices with modern scientific advancements.

The transformative potential of regenerative agriculture in India echoes across diverse landscapes and agricultural systems. From the terraced fields of Uttarakhand to the arid plains of Rajasthan, success stories emerge, demonstrating the efficacy of these practices. Farmers embracing regenerative methods witness tangible improvements such as increased soil fertility, enhanced crop yields, and reduced dependency on chemical inputs.

However, the journey towards widespread adoption of regenerative agriculture in India encounters hurdles. Accessibility to resources, education, and technical know-how pose challenges, particularly for smallholder farmers. Adapting regenerative practices across various agro-climatic zones while ensuring economic viability remains a daunting task. Yet, initiatives led by government bodies, NGOs, and grassroots organizations aim to bridge this gap, offering training, resources, and support to farmers.

The road ahead for regenerative agriculture in India demands a collective effort. Policymakers need to incentivize and support the transition toward these practices, while researchers continue to innovate and fine-tune methodologies suited to diverse farming contexts. Collaboration between stakeholders—farmers, consumers, researchers, and policymakers—is crucial to create an enabling environment that fosters the widespread adoption of regenerative agriculture.

In conclusion, the concept of regenerative agriculture encapsulates a holistic vision for farming—a vision that transcends mere sustenance to actively restore and rejuvenate the very ecosystems upon which agriculture depends. Its principles and practices hold the potential to revolutionize Indian agriculture, offering not just a means of sustainable production but a pathway toward ecological resilience and a thriving agricultural future.

Success Stories and Case Studies

Success stories and case studies from diverse regions of India stand as testament to the transformative power of regenerative agriculture. These real-life examples not only showcase the potential but also the tangible benefits that this approach brings to farmers and ecosystems across the country.

In the arid lands of Rajasthan, the story of Bhaskar Save, often termed the "Gandhi of Natural Farming," serves as an inspirational narrative. Save's farm, which spans 14 acres, stands as an oasis of biodiversity and abundance amidst the harsh desert landscape. His adoption of regenerative practices, including mixed cropping, composting, and water conservation techniques, transformed his farm into a thriving ecosystem. Save's methods not only increased productivity but also significantly reduced water usage, serving as a beacon for farmers grappling with water scarcity.

Moving south to Karnataka, the story of the Deccan Development Society (DDS) exemplifies community-led regenerative practices. In the Zaheerabad region, DDS initiated a movement empowering women farmer to embrace agroecological practices. By reviving traditional millet cultivation and integrating agroforestry with indigenous crops, DDS enabled farmers to enhance soil fertility, increase crop diversity, and improve nutritional outcomes. This initiative not only revitalized the land but also empowered local communities economically and socially.

In the northeastern state of Meghalaya, the practice of 'Jhum' cultivation, traditionally considered destructive due to slash-and-burn methods, underwent a transformation. The North East Slow Food and Agrobiodiversity Society (NESFAS) collaborated with indigenous communities to introduce regenerative agroecological practices. By implementing terracing, agroforestry, and diversified cropping systems, these communities witnessed a shift towards sustainable land use, preserving biodiversity, and ensuring food security while maintaining their cultural heritage.

Punjab, once synonymous with the Green Revolution, is experiencing a regenerative agriculture renaissance. Farmers like Amar Singh Virk, disillusioned with the ecological degradation caused by intensive chemical farming, turned to regenerative practices. Virk transitioned to organic farming and diversified his crops, integrating legumes and vegetables with traditional wheat and rice. Not only did this restore soil health, but it also enhanced biodiversity and reduced input costs, showcasing a viable alternative to the conventional high-input agriculture prevalent in the region.

The story of Araku Valley in Andhra Pradesh stands as a remarkable example of how regenerative agriculture uplifted tribal communities. Through the efforts of the Naandi Foundation, indigenous farming practices, including agroforestry and coffee cultivation, were revitalized. This initiative not only improved livelihoods by creating a sustainable source of income but also contributed to preserving the rich biodiversity of the region.

These success stories underscore the potential of regenerative agriculture to not only rejuvenate the land but also uplift communities, preserve traditional knowledge, and ensure food security in a changing climate. They stand as beacons guiding the way toward a more sustainable and resilient agricultural future for India.

Challenges

1. Limited Awareness and Education

- **Farmers' Knowledge Gap:** Many farmers lack awareness about regenerative practices, relying on conventional methods passed down through generations or promoted by agrochemical companies.
- **Educational Resources:** Access to credible information and educational resources about regenerative agriculture remains limited, especially in rural areas.

2. Access to Resources

- **Financial Constraints:** Smallholder farmers often lack financial resources to invest in new techniques or technologies associated with regenerative agriculture.
- **Availability of Inputs:** Accessibility to organic inputs, cover crops, diverse seed varieties, and compost may be limited or expensive, hindering adoption.

3. Land Tenure and Fragmentation

- **Small Land Holdings:** The prevalence of small and fragmented land holdings in India makes it challenging to implement holistic regenerative practices effectively.
- **Tenure Insecurity:** Farmers often lack secure land tenure, discouraging long-term investments in regenerative practices.

4. Water Scarcity and Irrigation Challenges

- **Erratic Rainfall Patterns:** Climate change-induced erratic weather patterns pose challenges in water management and irrigation, essential for regenerative practices.
- **Lack of Irrigation Infrastructure:** In regions with inadequate irrigation infrastructure, dry spells can significantly impact crop growth, affecting regenerative efforts.

5. Policy and Institutional Barriers

- **Inadequate Policy Support:** Agricultural policies often prioritize conventional farming methods and provide fewer incentives or support for regenerative agriculture.
- **Lack of Research and Extension Services:** Insufficient funding and attention to research and extension services focusing on regenerative agriculture limit its widespread adoption.

6. Market and Economic Challenges

- **Limited Market Access:** A lack of established markets or premiums for regenerative produce discourages farmers from transitioning to these methods.
- **Economic Viability:** Initial transition phases to regenerative practices might not immediately yield higher incomes, discouraging farmers from making the shift.

7. Resistance to Change

- **Mindset and Cultural Resistance:** Traditional mindsets and cultural practices deeply ingrained in farming communities may resist the adoption of newer, regenerative methods.
- **Risk Aversion:** Fear of crop failure or lower yields during the transition phase to regenerative practices dissuades risk-averse farmers.

8. Scaling Challenges

- **Adaptability to Different Agro-climatic Zones:** Strategies successful in one region might not seamlessly translate to other diverse agro-climatic zones in India.
- **Scaling Up Successful Models:** Challenges exist in replicating successful small-scale models of regenerative agriculture to larger landscapes.

9. Knowledge and Skill Gaps

- **Training and Technical Support:** Limited access to training programs and technical support hampers the ability of farmers to adopt regenerative techniques effectively.
- **Skill Development:** Enhancing skills in agroecology, soil management, and diverse cropping systems is essential but often lacking.

Addressing these challenges demands a concerted effort from multiple stakeholders. Policymakers must formulate supportive policies, providing financial incentives, extension services, and research support for regenerative agriculture. NGOs and community organizations can play a pivotal role in disseminating knowledge, providing training, and facilitating access to resources. Collaboration between private sector entities, research institutions, and farmers' collectives can innovate scalable solutions tailored to diverse agricultural landscapes, ensuring a smoother transition toward regenerative practices.

Opportunities:Top of Form

1. Enhanced Soil Health and Fertility

- **Carbon Sequestration:** Regenerative practices such as cover cropping and minimal tillage enhance soil organic matter, contributing to carbon sequestration and mitigating climate change.
- **Improved Water Retention:** Healthy soils under regenerative practices have improved water retention capacities, crucial in drought-prone areas, reducing dependence on irrigation.

2. Biodiversity Conservation

- **Preservation of Native Species:** Regenerative agriculture emphasizes crop diversity, preserving indigenous plant varieties, and fostering biodiversity, contributing to ecosystem resilience.
- **Habitat Restoration:** Practices like agroforestry create habitats for beneficial insects and wildlife, promoting ecological balance.

3. Climate Resilience

- **Adaptation to Climate Change:** Diverse crop rotations and resilient farming methods under regenerative agriculture better equip farms to withstand extreme weather events and erratic rainfall patterns.
- **Reduced Carbon Footprint:** Sequestration of carbon in the soil contributes to mitigating greenhouse gas emissions, a critical step in combating climate change.

4. Resource Conservation and Efficiency

- **Water Conservation:** Implementing regenerative practices leads to reduced water usage through improved soil structure, minimizing runoff and optimizing water retention.
- **Reduced Chemical Dependency:** Transitioning away from synthetic inputs reduces environmental pollution and improves the health of ecosystems.

5. Economic Viability and Farmer Prosperity

- **Increased Resilience to Market Fluctuations:** Diversification of crops and reduced input costs make farmers less susceptible to market volatilities, enhancing their economic resilience.
- **Long-term Cost Savings:** Once established, regenerative systems require fewer external inputs, reducing farmers' dependency on costly chemicals and fertilizers.

6. Community Empowerment and Social Impact

- **Enhanced Food Security:** Diverse cropping systems and improved soil fertility contribute to food security by ensuring a variety of nutritious produce for communities.

- **Empowerment of Smallholders:** Regenerative practices can empower smallholder farmers by improving their self-sufficiency and resilience to external shocks.

7. Market Opportunities and Consumer Demand

- **Rising Demand for Sustainable Produce:** Growing global and domestic demand for sustainably produced food presents market opportunities for farmers adopting regenerative practices.
- **Premium Pricing:** Certifications and labels associated with regenerative agriculture can attract premium prices in niche markets, incentivizing farmers.

8. Technological Innovations and Knowledge Sharing

- **Digital Solutions:** Technological advancements offer tools like precision agriculture, remote sensing, and data analytics, aiding in the implementation and monitoring of regenerative practices.
- **Knowledge Exchange Platforms:** Online platforms and farmer networks facilitate the sharing of best practices, fostering a community of learning and collaboration.

9. Policy Support and Government Initiatives

- **Incentive Schemes:** Governments can introduce subsidies, grants, and incentives for farmers adopting regenerative practices, encouraging wider adoption.
- **Capacity Building:** Investment in research, extension services, and farmer training programs can bridge knowledge gaps and promote the uptake of regenerative agriculture.

Harnessing these opportunities requires collaborative efforts from various stakeholders—governments, NGOs, research institutions, farmers, and consumers. By capitalizing on these prospects, India can pave the way for a resilient, sustainable, and prosperous agricultural future through regenerative practices.

The Road Ahead

1. Policy Reforms and Supportive Frameworks

- **Policy Alignment:** Government policies need alignment to promote and incentivize regenerative practices, offering subsidies, tax breaks, and financial assistance.
- **Research and Development Funding:** Increased funding for research institutions to study and develop regenerative agriculture techniques suited to diverse agro-climatic zones.

2. Education and Awareness

- **Farmer Outreach Programs:** Conducting extensive farmer education programs, workshops, and demonstrations to impart knowledge and build confidence in adopting regenerative methods.
- **Curriculum Integration:** Incorporating regenerative agriculture principles into formal agricultural education curriculums to train the next generation of farmers.

3. Technological Integration and Innovation

- **Tech Adoption:** Encouraging the use of precision farming technologies, remote sensing, and digital tools to optimize regenerative practices and improve efficiency.
- **Innovation Hubs:** Establishing innovation hubs or centers to foster research, experimentation, and dissemination of innovative regenerative techniques.

4. Financial Support and Market Access

- **Access to Finance:** Facilitating access to credit and microfinance for smallholder farmers to invest in transitioning to regenerative methods and purchasing necessary resources.
- **Market Linkages:** Developing robust market linkages and creating demand for regeneratively produced goods to ensure fair prices and economic viability for farmers.

5. Capacity Building and Skill Development

- **Training Programs:** Scaling up training programs, field schools, and knowledge-sharing platforms to equip farmers with the skills and technical know-how needed for regenerative agriculture.
- **Extension Services:** Strengthening extension services to provide ongoing support, advice, and troubleshooting for farmers transitioning to regenerative practices.

6. Promotion of Farmer Cooperatives and Networks

- **Collective Action:** Encouraging the formation of farmer cooperatives and networks to facilitate collective learning, resource-sharing, and joint implementation of regenerative practices.
- **Community-Led Initiatives:** Supporting community-led initiatives that promote regenerative agriculture and empower local farmers to drive the change.

7. Ecosystem-Based Approaches and Partnerships

- **Ecosystem Integration:** Emphasizing integrated approaches that connect agriculture with wider ecosystems, promoting biodiversity conservation, and ecosystem restoration.

- **Multi-stakeholder Partnerships:** Fostering partnerships between government bodies, NGOs, private sector entities, and research institutions to leverage expertise and resources.

8. Monitoring, Evaluation, and Knowledge Exchange

- **Monitoring and Evaluation Systems:** Establishing robust monitoring and evaluation mechanisms to track the impact of regenerative practices on soil health, biodiversity, and farmer livelihoods.
- **Knowledge Exchange Platforms:** Encouraging platforms for sharing success stories, lessons learned, and best practices among stakeholders to facilitate learning and replication.

9. Scaling Successful Models and Replication

- **Replication Programs:** Identifying successful regenerative models and scaling them across different regions, adapting them to suit local contexts and agroecological conditions.
- **Demonstration Farms:** Establishing demonstration farms to showcase the viability and benefits of regenerative agriculture, encouraging wider adoption through practical examples.

10. Cultural Shift and Social Acceptance

- **Awareness Campaigns:** Conducting widespread awareness campaigns to shift societal attitudes towards valuing and supporting regenerative agriculture.
- **Cultural Integration:** Integrating regenerative principles with local cultural beliefs and practices, emphasizing the cultural significance of sustainable farming.

The road ahead for regenerative agriculture in India demands a holistic approach, blending policy reforms, technological innovations, capacity building, and strong community engagement. Collaboration among stakeholders and sustained commitment are vital to traverse this path toward a resilient, sustainable, and prosperous agricultural future.

Conclusion

In conclusion, the trajectory toward regenerative agriculture in India represents not just a farming paradigm but a profound shift in how we perceive our relationship with the land. It's a journey weaving traditional wisdom with modern innovation, forging a path toward ecological restoration, agricultural resilience, and farmer prosperity. As India navigates the complexities of food security, climate change, and dwindling natural resources, regenerative agriculture emerges as a beacon of hope. The future hinges on collaborative efforts, aligning policies, empowering farmers with knowledge and resources, and fostering a culture that values sustainability. By nurturing the soil, preserving biodiversity, and embracing practices that respect the rhythms of nature, India can steer its agricultural landscape toward vitality and resilience, ensuring a legacy of abundance for generations to come. Regenerative agriculture offers not just a solution to agricultural challenges but a promise of harmonious coexistence with our environment.

References

Alok, R. (2011). A uniform decimal code for growth stages of crops and weeds, *Annals of Applied Biology*, pp.561–601.

Bernard, T. and David, J. S. (2009). Reaching the rural poor through rural producer organizations: A study of agricultural marketing cooperatives in Ethiopia, *Food Policy*, pp. 60-69.

Elsner, J. E., Smith, C. W. & Owen, O. F. (2019). Uniform stage descriptions in upland cotton, *Crop Science,* pp. 361–363.

Haun, J. R. (2013). Visual quantification of wheat development. *Agronomy Journal,* pp. 116–119.

Moore, K. J., Moser, L. E., Vogel, K. P., Waller, S. S., Johnson, B. E. & Pedersen, J. F. (2021). Describing and quantifying growth stages of perennial forage grasses, *Agronomy Journal,* pp. 1073–1077.

Stockbridge, M. A. and Dorward, J. (2023). Farmer Organizations for Market Access: Learning from Success, *Briefing Paper*, pp. 34-45.

Trebbin, A., and Hassler, M. (2012). Farmers' producer companies in India: a new concept for collective action, *Environment and Planning*, 44(2), 411-427.

5

Challenges and Opportunities in Global Food Security

Subhashree Mishra

PhD Scholar, Department of Agricultural Economics, Institute of Agricultural Sciences, SOA, Bhubaneswar

Abstract

Global food security confronts a nexus of challenges encompassing population growth, climate change, resource constraints, and socioeconomic disparities. This chapter meticulously dissects these complexities, delving into their ramifications on agricultural landscapes, community well-being, and the intricate web of food systems worldwide. From the nuanced exploration of technological innovations to the critical examination of policy interventions, each facet converges to illuminate pathways toward a more secure and sustainable food future. Insights into gender equality in agriculture, urban farming's resilience, and cultural dietary patterns add depth to the discourse. Propelled by innovation, collaboration, and inclusivity, solutions emerge: empowering communities, fostering equitable access, and preserving cultural diversity. The chapter's narrative unfolds as a beacon of hope, advocating for collective action, education, and policy reform. Together, these efforts aspire to sculpt a world where nourishment transcends boundaries, forging a resilient and equitable global food ecosystem.

Introduction

In an era defined by unprecedented connectivity and shared global challenges, the assurance of food security emerges as a cornerstone of human welfare and societal stability. At its core, the concept of global food security embodies a delicate equilibrium—wherein the abundant availability, accessibility, utilization, and consistency of nutritious sustenance are assured for all. Yet, this equilibrium remains precariously fragile amidst a confluence of modern predicaments. The imperatives of nourishment transcend mere sustenance; they intertwine with the fabric of public health, economic fortitude, and societal harmony. The imperious need to address food security issues stems from the stark realities it imposes: a profound impact on individual health, the stifling of economic prosperity, and the potential for social unrest. As the global populace burgeons and the specter of climate change looms ominously over agricultural landscapes, this chapter embarks on a multifaceted exploration. Within these pages, we delve into the intricate tapestry of challenges and opportunities shaping the discourse on global food security. By peering into this mosaic of complexities, our intent is to illuminate viable pathways toward fostering a more resilient, inclusive, and sustainable food ecosystem, one that ensures nourishment and stability for all corners of the globe.

Challenges in Achieving Food Security

Population Growth

- **Impact on Food Demand**: With an ever-expanding global population, estimated to reach 9 billion by 2050, the demand for food surges. This population growth exerts tremendous pressure on agricultural systems to produce more while competing for land, water, and resources.
- **Strain on Resources**: Meeting this escalating demand requires intensified agricultural practices, leading to increased land use, deforestation, and overexploitation of water resources. These activities often contribute to environmental degradation, exacerbating the challenges faced by farmers.

Climate Change

- **Disrupting Agricultural Patterns**: Climate change disrupts traditional weather patterns, leading to irregular rainfall, prolonged droughts, and extreme weather events. These changes negatively impact crop yields, threaten livestock, and increase the vulnerability of small-scale farmers, particularly in regions already susceptible to environmental fluctuations.
- **Loss of Arable Land**: Rising temperatures and erratic weather conditions jeopardize arable land, either through desertification, soil erosion, or salinization. This loss diminishes the available land for cultivation, thereby limiting global food production potential.

Resource Scarcity

- **Diminishing Water Resources**: Agriculture consumes a substantial portion of the world's freshwater resources. However, water scarcity due to over-extraction, pollution, and inefficient irrigation practices poses a significant challenge to sustaining agricultural output.
- **Soil Degradation and Biodiversity Loss**: Soil erosion, nutrient depletion, and loss of biodiversity further compound the challenge. Unsustainable agricultural practices contribute to soil degradation, reducing fertility and compromising the long-term productivity of farmlands.

Food Waste and Loss

- **Inefficiencies in Supply Chain:** Approximately one-third of the food produced for human consumption is lost or wasted globally. This waste occurs throughout the supply chain, from production and harvest to distribution and consumption, exacerbated by inadequate infrastructure, storage facilities, and logistical inefficiencies.

Each of these challenges intersects and amplifies the complexities of achieving global food security. Addressing these issues necessitates comprehensive strategies that consider sustainable agricultural practices, resource management, and innovative solutions to minimize waste and enhance efficiency throughout the food supply chain.

Socioeconomic Factors and Access to Food

Income Disparities

- **Impact on Food Access**: Income inequality significantly influences access to quality food. Lower-income households often allocate a larger proportion of their earnings to food purchases, limiting their ability to afford nutritious options. This disparity exacerbates the prevalence of food insecurity among marginalized populations.
- **Nutritional Disparities**: Higher-priced nutritious food items, such as fresh fruits and vegetables, become less accessible to economically disadvantaged individuals, leading to imbalances in dietary quality and health outcomes.

Rural-Urban Disparities

- **Infrastructure Challenges**: Rural areas face infrastructural limitations, including inadequate transportation networks and storage facilities. This deficiency impedes the efficient movement of food from farms to markets, affecting both food availability and affordability.
- **Access to Markets**: Urban areas often have better access to diverse food options due to proximity to markets and supermarkets. Conversely, rural communities might have limited access, relying heavily on local produce, which might not always meet dietary requirements.

Conflict and Food Insecurity

- **Disruption of Food Systems**: Conflict-ridden regions experience disruptions in food production, distribution, and access. Displacement of populations, destruction of agricultural infrastructure, and trade blockades exacerbate food insecurity, leading to acute shortages and malnutrition.
- **Humanitarian Challenges**: Conflict zones often pose immense challenges for humanitarian aid and relief efforts, hindering the delivery of essential food supplies to affected populations.

Addressing socioeconomic disparities in food access requires holistic approaches encompassing policy interventions, targeted assistance programs, and initiatives aimed at improving infrastructure, livelihoods, and market access in marginalized communities. Moreover, resolving conflicts and fostering stability in regions prone to unrest are pivotal for ensuring sustained access to food for affected populations.

Technological Innovations and Solutions

Precision Agriculture

- **Optimizing Resource Use**: Precision agriculture employs technology like GPS, sensors, and drones to collect data on soil conditions, moisture levels, and crop health. This data-driven approach enables farmers to apply resources—water, fertilizers, and pesticides—more precisely, reducing waste and environmental impact while maximizing yields.
- **Enhancing Crop Management**: By utilizing real-time data analytics, farmers can make informed decisions about planting schedules, pest management, and irrigation, thereby improving overall crop health and productivity.

Biotechnology and GMOs

- **Increased Crop Resilience**: Biotechnological advancements have led to the development of genetically modified organisms (GMOs) with traits like drought tolerance, pest resistance, and increased nutritional value. These modifications bolster crop resilience against environmental stressors and pests, potentially enhancing yields.
- **Controversies and Considerations**: However, GMOs also evoke debates surrounding safety, ethics, and their long-term environmental impact. Balancing the benefits with ethical and environmental concerns remains a critical aspect of utilizing biotechnology for food security.

Data Analytics and AI

- **Optimizing Farming Practices**: Data analytics and artificial intelligence empower farmers to make data-driven decisions, optimizing crop selection, planting techniques, and resource allocation. Machine learning algorithms analyze vast datasets to predict crop diseases, optimize irrigation, and suggest optimal harvesting times.
- **Supply Chain Efficiency**: AI-driven technologies enhance supply chain management by predicting demand patterns, optimizing logistics, and reducing food waste through better inventory management and distribution strategies.

Technological innovations hold immense promise in addressing various challenges associated with global food security. However, their effective implementation requires consideration of ethical concerns, equitable access to technology for all farmers, and a comprehensive understanding of local contexts and environmental impacts. Integrating these innovations into sustainable agricultural practices can significantly contribute to improving food production efficiency and resilience.

Policy Interventions and Collaborative Efforts

Government Policies

- **Agricultural Subsidies and Support:** Governments implement policies like subsidies, agricultural extension programs, and investment in rural infrastructure to support farmers. These measures aim to enhance agricultural productivity, improve access to markets, and provide financial assistance to mitigate risks.
- **Food Distribution Programs**: Governments often institute food assistance programs, such as school feeding programs or food stamps, to ensure vulnerable populations have access to nutritious food.

International Cooperation

- **Global Initiatives and Partnerships:** International organizations, NGOs, and governments collaborate on initiatives like the UN's Sustainable Development Goals (SDGs) or the World Food Programme (WFP). These collaborations focus on enhancing food security through knowledge sharing, capacity building, and financial support to vulnerable regions.
- **Trade Policies and Aid Programs:** International trade agreements and aid programs facilitate the movement of food across borders, aiding regions facing shortages. Aid programs also support agricultural development and emergency relief efforts in food-insecure areas.

Community Empowerment

- **Promoting Sustainable Practices:** Engaging local communities in sustainable farming practices, such as agroforestry or conservation agriculture, enhances food production while preserving natural resources.
- **Education and Capacity Building:** Empowering communities through education on nutrition, agricultural techniques, and entrepreneurship fosters self-reliance and resilience against food insecurity.

The role of policy interventions and collaborative efforts is pivotal in addressing systemic challenges associated with food security. Effective policies, both at national and international levels, coupled with collaborative initiatives, contribute to building resilient food systems and ensuring equitable access to food for all populations. Empowering communities through education and sustainable practices further strengthens the foundation for long-term food security.

Future Prospects and Recommendations

Role of Innovation

- **Emerging Technologies**: Novel advancements like vertical farming, aquaponics, and lab-grown meat hold promise in revolutionizing food production. Vertical farming, for instance, utilizes indoor facilities with controlled environments to grow crops vertically, maximizing space and reducing resource usage.
- **Sustainability Focus**: Innovations must prioritize sustainability, emphasizing eco-friendly practices to minimize environmental impact while meeting increasing food demands.

Educational Initiatives

- **Promoting Food Literacy**: Educational programs focusing on nutrition, food systems, and sustainable practices can instill better food choices, reducing food waste and improving health outcomes.
- **Empowering Future Generations**: Integrating food education into school curriculums cultivates an understanding of the food system's complexities and the importance of sustainable practices among younger generations.

Advocacy and Engagement

- **Stakeholder Collaboration:** Engaging diverse stakeholders—governments, NGOs, businesses, farmers, and consumers—in dialogues and collaborative efforts fosters collective responsibility and innovative solutions.
- **Consumer Awareness:** Raising awareness among consumers about the impact of their choices on food systems encourages more sustainable consumption patterns, reducing waste and supporting ethical practices.

The future of global food security hinges on the conscientious integration of innovative technologies, educational initiatives, and widespread stakeholder engagement. Prioritizing sustainable innovations, educating future generations, and fostering collaboration among stakeholders can pave the way for resilient and equitable food systems capable of meeting the challenges of tomorrow.

Socio-Cultural Perspectives on Dietary Patterns

Diversity in Dietary Patterns

- **Cultural Influences**: Dietary habits and food preferences vary significantly across cultures and regions, influencing consumption patterns. Understanding and respecting cultural diversity in food choices is essential in crafting sustainable food security solutions.
- **Nutritional Diversity**: Encouraging diverse dietary patterns, incorporating local and traditional foods rich in nutrients, can enhance resilience against food insecurity. Emphasizing the nutritional value of indigenous crops fosters both food security and cultural preservation.

Community-Based Approaches

- **Promoting Local Food Systems**: Empowering local food systems preserves cultural heritage while ensuring access to nutritious foods. Supporting small-scale farmers and local markets strengthens community resilience and food sovereignty.
- **Inclusive Policies**: Developing policies that consider cultural diversity in dietary needs and promote the integration of traditional foods into broader food systems fosters inclusivity and sustainability.

Challenges and Opportunities

- **Balancing Modernization and Tradition**: Encouraging traditional diets amidst globalization poses challenges. Finding a balance that respects cultural heritage while embracing innovation is crucial for sustaining diverse and nutritious food systems.
- **Education and Awareness**: Educating communities about the nutritional value of traditional foods, promoting culinary diversity, and fostering appreciation for cultural heritage can create opportunities for sustainable food practices.

Understanding and integrating socio-cultural perspectives into food security initiatives is crucial for fostering inclusive and resilient food systems. Embracing diverse dietary patterns not only ensures nutritional adequacy but also respects and preserves cultural identities, contributing to the overall well-being of communities worldwide.

Gender Equality in Agricultural Practices

Women in Agriculture

- **Contribution to Food Production:** Women play a crucial role in agricultural production, comprising a significant portion of the agricultural workforce globally. They contribute to various tasks, from planting and harvesting to processing and marketing crops.
- **Access to Resources**: Despite their pivotal role, women often face constraints in accessing land, credit, technology, and agricultural extension services. Addressing these disparities is crucial for enhancing agricultural productivity and food security.

Empowerment and Decision-Making

- **Educational Opportunities**: Providing education and training opportunities for women in agriculture improves their skills, knowledge, and decision-making abilities. This empowerment fosters more sustainable and productive agricultural practices.

- **Land Rights and Ownership**: Ensuring women's access to and ownership of land empowers them economically and enhances their ability to invest in agriculture, contributing to increased food production.

Policy and Support Mechanisms

- **Gender-Inclusive Policies**: Implementing policies that promote gender equality in agriculture, such as equitable land rights and access to resources, is vital. These policies can enable women to participate more effectively in decision-making processes and benefit from agricultural development initiatives.
- **Supportive Programs**: Introducing programs tailored to women in agriculture, such as credit facilities, extension services, and technology training, strengthens their capacity to contribute to food security.

Gender equality in agriculture is not only a matter of social justice but also a fundamental aspect of ensuring food security and sustainable development. Empowering women in agriculture through education, access to resources, and supportive policies can significantly enhance agricultural productivity and contribute to global food security efforts.

Urban Agriculture and Food Resilience

Urban Agriculture Initiatives

- **Utilizing Urban Spaces**: Urban agriculture involves cultivating crops, raising livestock, or producing food within urban areas. Utilizing rooftops, community gardens, vacant lots, and vertical farming, it contributes to local food production.
- **Enhancing Food Accessibility**: Urban agriculture initiatives reduce food miles, providing fresh produce closer to consumers. This accessibility improves food security, especially in urban areas with limited access to affordable and nutritious food.

Environmental Sustainability

- **Green Spaces and Biodiversity**: Urban agriculture encourages the creation of green spaces, promoting biodiversity and mitigating the urban heat island effect. It contributes to environmental sustainability by reducing carbon footprint and fostering local ecosystems.
- **Waste Reduction**: These initiatives often incorporate composting and recycling practices, minimizing organic waste and creating a closed-loop system that enhances resource efficiency.

Community Engagement and Resilience

- **Community Empowerment**: Urban agriculture fosters community engagement and social cohesion by involving residents in food production. It educates communities about food systems and encourages healthy eating habits.

- **Resilience in Crisis**: During times of crisis or disruptions in global supply chains, urban agriculture serves as a resilient alternative, ensuring a local supply of fresh produce and reducing dependence on distant sources.

Policy and Infrastructural Support

- **Supportive Policies**: Municipal policies that promote and facilitate urban agriculture, such as zoning regulations and land-use policies, are essential. Supportive measures encourage and sustain these initiatives within urban landscapes.
- **Infrastructure Development**: Investing in infrastructure, such as community gardens, educational programs, and accessible green spaces, provides the necessary framework for the success of urban agriculture initiatives.

Urban agriculture contributes significantly to enhancing food resilience, environmental sustainability, and community engagement in urban settings. Encouraging and supporting these initiatives through policy frameworks and infrastructural development can strengthen local food systems and contribute to broader efforts towards global food security.

Conclusion

In the labyrinthine discourse of global food security, a mosaic of challenges and opportunities converges, demanding concerted action and innovative solutions. The journey through these intricacies has illuminated the daunting hurdles: from population expansion and climate tumults to socioeconomic disparities and resource scarcities. However, amidst these challenges lies a tapestry woven with threads of hope and resilience. The multifaceted nature of food security demands a holistic approach, acknowledging the interconnectedness of agricultural practices, socioeconomic structures, technological advancements, and cultural nuances. Initiatives must embrace precision agriculture's data-driven efficiency, biotechnology's potential, and AI's analytical prowess while preserving cultural dietary diversity and empowering marginalized voices. Collaboration at both local and global levels, underpinned by inclusive policies and community engagement, forms the bedrock of sustainable solutions. Empowerment emerges not just as a concept but as an imperative—empowering farmers, women in agriculture, urban communities, and local food systems. Education, equitable access to resources, and policy frameworks promoting gender equality and urban agriculture stand as catalysts for change. As the world navigates the complex terrain of the 21st century, the clarion call resounds louder than ever: a call for collective action, innovation, and solidarity. Together, through visionary policies, technological innovations, community engagement, and an unwavering commitment to equity, we can forge a future where food security is not an elusive dream but a tangible reality for every individual, in every corner of the globe. The journey toward a more nourished, resilient, and equitable world begins today.

References

Little, T. M. (1978). If Galileo Published in HortScience. *HortScience* 13, 504–506.

Nelson, L. A. & Rawlings, J. O. (1983). Ten common misuses of statistics in agronomic research and reporting. Journal of Agronomic Education, 12, 100–105.

Neuendorf, K. K. E., Mehl, J. P., Jr. & Jackson, J. A. (2011). Glossary of Geology (5th ed., revised). American Geosciences Institute.

Sanderson, M. A. (1992). Morphological development of switchgrass and kleingrass. Agronomy Journal, 84,415–419.

Schneiter, A. A. & Miller, J. F. (1981). Description of sunflower growth stages. *Crop Science*, 21, 901–903.

Seddigh, M. & Jolliff, G.D. (1988). Recommendations on preparation of line graphs for presentation of scientific data. *Journal of Agronomic Education,* 17, 3–6.

Segel, I. H. (1976). Biochemical calculations: How to solve mathematical problems in general biochemistry (2nd ed.). Wiley.

Thien, S. J. & Oster, J. D. (1981). The international system of units and its particular application to soil chemistry. *Journal of Agronomic Education*, 10, 62–70.

Tomlin, C. D. S. (Ed.). (2011). The pesticide manual: A world compendium (15th ed.). British Crop Protection Council, 501–503.

6

Technology Advancements and Digital Transformation in Extension: Integrating AI and IoT in Agricultural Extension

[1]Guru Prasad Satapathy and [2]Sidharth Dash

[1]Odisha University of Agriculture & Technology, Bhubaneswar, Odisha
[2](Livelihood), CBSAE Dev. Project, Odisha University of Agriculture & Technology, Bhubaneswar, Odisha

Abstract

With a focus on the fusion of artificial intelligence (AI) and the Internet of Things (IoT), this chapter discusses the dynamic landscape of technological breakthroughs and digital change in agricultural extension. It begins by outlining the development of agricultural extension services across time and emphasizes the role that technology has played in changing this industry. IoT is emphasized for its real-time data gathering and monitoring capabilities, while AI is investigated for its capacity to analyze data, provide decision assistance, and promote automation. By highlighting their roles in precision agriculture, real-time monitoring, and sustainable agricultural techniques, it highlights the synergistic potential of integrating AI and IoT in extension services. Along with chances to address them, issues including data privacy, accessibility, and economic sustainability are examined. A call to action is issued to extension practitioners and policymakers, highlighting the need for collaboration, digital literacy, privacy regulation, and investment. The integration of AI and IoT holds the promise of a more prosperous and sustainable future in agriculture, made possible by technology's transformative power.

Keywords: *Agricultural Extension, Technology Advancements, Digital Transformation, Artificial Intelligence (AI), Internet of Things (IoT)*

1. Introduction

A key element in the world of agriculture, agricultural extension has long been seen as the link between scientific knowledge and the practical needs of farmers. This chapter examines how technological advancements, particularly those related to artificial intelligence (AI) and the internet of things (IoT), are fundamentally altering agricultural extension services and the agricultural industry as a whole.

1.1 Definition of Agricultural Extension

The process of sharing knowledge, information, and innovations with farmers and rural communities in order to enhance their agricultural practices and, in turn, their livelihoods, is known as agricultural extension. In the past, face-to-face interactions between extension workers and farmers were a major component of extension services. These encounters included the exchange of knowledge about pest management, livestock care, crop management, and sustainable farming methods. Unquestionably, traditional extension techniques have contributed to boosting agricultural productivity and reducing poverty in rural regions.

1.2 Significance of Technology in Extension

It is impossible to emphasize the importance of technology in agricultural extension. The generation, dissemination, and use of agricultural knowledge could all be revolutionized by technology. The requirement for real-time, data-driven decision-making as well as resource limitations and restricted reach are some of the recurrent issues traditional extension services confront.

In the context of extension, technology plays several pivotal roles:

1. **Access to Information:** Farmers can now access knowledge resources from anywhere thanks to technology, particularly the internet and mobile devices, which have increased access to agricultural information.
2. **Data-Driven Decision-Making:** Huge volumes of agricultural data can be collected and analyzed thanks to advanced technologies, which empowers farmers to decide wisely about crop management, resource allocation, and market opportunities..
3. **Precision Agriculture:** With the help of technology, farmers may employ precision agriculture to better utilize resources and minimize waste by accurately tailoring their operations to the demands of their crops or livestock.
4. **Scalability:** Extension services are more scalable and affordable thanks to digital platforms and technologies since they have the ability to reach a considerably bigger audience than conventional face-to-face extension methods.

1.3 Overview of AI and IoT in Agriculture

Understanding Artificial Intelligence (AI) and the Internet of Things (IoT) is crucial for appreciating the transformative potential of technology in agricultural extension.

Artificial Intelligence (AI): Artificial intelligence (AI) is the replication of human intellect in machines, allowing them to analyze data, draw conclusions, and carry out actions that ordinarily call for human intelligence. AI is being utilized in agriculture to create disease-prediction models for crops, improve planting schedules, and even manage autonomous farming machinery.

The Internet of Things (IoT): The Internet of Things (IoT) is a network of physically connected gadgets, machinery, structures, and other items that are equipped with sensors, software, and network connectivity. These gadgets gather and exchange data, giving useful insights instantly. IoT devices are utilized in agriculture for a variety of tasks, including tracking animal health, monitoring soil moisture levels, and managing irrigation systems.

2.1 Digital Transformation in Agricultural Extension

Historical Perspective

The continuous digital transition is set against the fascinating backdrop of the historical development of agricultural extension services. Face-to-face contacts between extension agents and farmers have always been the hallmark of extension services. These exchanges were essential for the spread of knowledge because they provided farmers with advice on the best ways to cultivate crops, manage their livestock, and control pests. The extension agents served as bridges between the rural community and the research organizations.

2.2 The Need for Digital Transformation

A number of interrelated challenges, such as the need to secure food security, resource limitations, climate change, and global population expansion, have combined to create the need for digital transformation in agricultural extension. Due to these difficulties, extension services must adopt a more data-driven, scalable, and flexible strategy. Here are some reasons why digital transformation is vital:

1. **Scalability:** Even though they are valuable, traditional extension programs have difficulty reaching a large and diversified farming population. Because of their scalability, digital technologies enable extension services to reach a wider audience, especially in isolated or underserved locations.

2. **Timeliness:** Making timely judgments about things like planting and irrigation schedules is crucial to agriculture. Real-time data is made available through digital tools, so that farmers have access to the most recent information for making decisions.

3. **Customization:** Agricultural demands and difficulties vary by region. With the help of digital technologies, extension services can be tailored to meet the needs of particular farms and local conditions.
4. **Efficiency:** The administrative burden on extension agents is reduced by the use of digital tools, allowing them to concentrate more on providing advising services. Better outcomes and better resource allocation are the results of this efficiency.

2.3 Benefits and Objectives

Digital transformation in agricultural extension offers a multitude of benefits and aligns with several key objectives:

1. **Improved Access to Information:** Farmers have quick access to a multitude of agricultural information, such as weather forecasts, market pricing, and best practices, thanks to digital platforms and mobile applications. Farmers are now able to make more informed decisions thanks to the democratization of information.
2. **Enhanced Decision Support:** AI-driven decision support systems examine data and provide farmers with tailored recommendations. These systems, for instance, can recommend ideal planting times or prescribe certain pest control methods, enhancing crop yields and resource effectiveness.
3. **Increased Agricultural Productivity:** Extension services can assist farmers in implementing precision agriculture methods by utilizing technology, which will increase yields, decrease resource waste, and improve sustainability.
4. **Empowering Rural Communities:** By giving farmers in isolated places access to markets, financial services, and agricultural knowledge, digital transformation promotes economic inclusion. Rural development and poverty reduction are both aided by this empowerment.
5. **Sustainability:** For the protection of the ecosystem, sustainable farming methods are essential. Environmental indicators can be monitored using digital instruments, which makes it easier to adopt eco-friendly farming practices.

3.1 Artificial Intelligence (AI) in Agricultural Extension

Through the provision of creative solutions that facilitate decision-making, optimize resource management, and raise overall agricultural output, artificial intelligence (AI) is transforming agricultural extension services. With an emphasis on its applications in data analysis, decision support systems, and crop management, which are demonstrated through case studies, this section examines the role of AI in agriculture.

3.2 Understanding AI in Agriculture

AI, in the context of agriculture, refers to the deployment of algorithms and machine learning techniques to process vast amounts of data from various sources, such as satellite imagery, weather stations, soil sensors, and farm machinery. Here's an overview of AI's significance in agriculture:

- **Data Integration:** AI systems are able to smoothly combine data from many sources, giving a comprehensive picture of the farming ecosystem. This connection makes detailed analysis and insights possible.
- **Predictive Analytics:** With the aid of artificial intelligence (AI), it is feasible to forecast crop yields, spot disease outbreaks, and determine market pricing with accuracy based on past data.
- **Automation:** Planting, harvesting, and weeding operations are all automated by robotics and machinery powered by AI. This lowers labour expenses and improves farming operations' precision.
- **Real-time Monitoring:** Real-time environmental monitoring is made possible by AI systems, enabling farmers to react quickly to changing situations like abrupt weather changes.

3.3 AI-Powered Data Analysis: One of AI's key strengths lies in its ability to analyze vast datasets quickly and accurately, a task that would be challenging for humans. In agriculture, this capability translates into:

- **Crop Health Monitoring:** AI systems can assess crop health, spot symptoms of stress or disease, and suggest time-sensitive remedies by analysing satellite pictures and data from drones.
- **Soil Analysis:** AI-driven soil sensors can measure the moisture content, nutrient levels, and soil quality, giving farmers useful information for the best irrigation and fertilization practices.
- **Pest and Disease Identification:** By examining photos of plants, AI-powered image recognition systems may spot pests, illnesses, and nutrient deficits. Early detection aids in reducing crop losses.

3.4 AI in Decision Support Systems

AI plays a pivotal role in decision support systems that assist farmers in making informed choices. These systems leverage AI's capabilities to:

- **Generate Recommendations:** Farmers can get individualized guidance on planting dates, crop rotations, and pest control techniques from AI-driven recommendation engines.
- **Risk Assessment:** Farmers can select the most appropriate and sustainable solutions by using AI models to evaluate the financial and environmental risks related to various farming operations.

- **Market Analysis:** AI can analyze market trends and price fluctuations, helping farmers decide when and where to sell their produce for maximum profit.

3.5 Case Studies: AI in Crop Management

Case Study 1: Precision Irrigation with AI

Precision irrigation is essential in areas with scarce water supplies. AI-driven systems, like the one used in the Central Valley of California, employ weather information and soil moisture sensors to accurately control irrigation. This lowers the need for water, saves resources, and increases agricultural yields.

Case Study 2: Disease Detection with Computer Vision

- In India, AI-based image recognition systems have been deployed to detect crop diseases early. Farmers can take action promptly to prevent disease spread and minimize crop losses. This technology is especially valuable for smallholder farmers who lack access to traditional extension services.

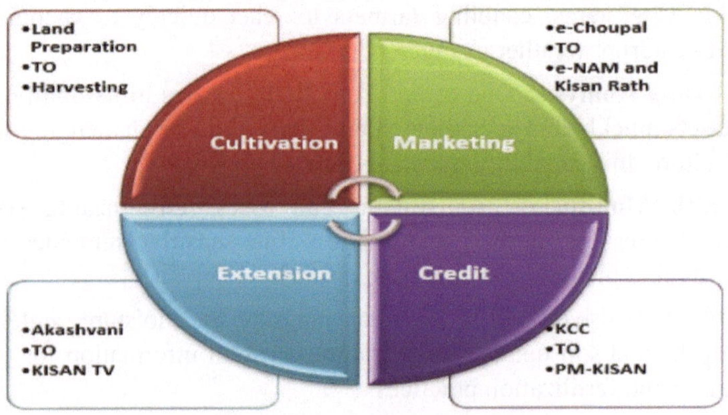

Fig. 1: Source: https://optimizeias.com/e-technology-in-aid-of-farmers/

4.1 The Internet of Things (IoT) in Agricultural Extension

In the area of agricultural extension, the Internet of Things (IoT) has turned the tide. It provides real-time data collecting and monitoring capabilities to farmers and extension agencies, enabling precision agriculture and sustainable farming methods. We delve into the importance of IoT in agriculture in this area, with a focus on real-time monitoring, sustainable agricultural methods, and case studies demonstrating its use in livestock management.

4.2 IoT and Precision Agriculture

Precision agriculture aims to optimize farming practices by tailoring them to specific field conditions, ultimately increasing productivity and resource efficiency. IoT is instrumental in achieving precision agriculture by:

- **Sensor Deployment:** Data is gathered from the field via IoT devices that are outfitted with a variety of sensors, including soil moisture monitors, weather stations, and GPS trackers.
- **Data Integration:** A thorough picture of field conditions, including soil quality, moisture content, temperature, and other factors, is produced using data from IoT devices that has been combined and analysed.
- **Actionable Insights:** Farmers are able to make accurate judgments concerning pest management, fertilizer, and irrigation because to these insights. Farmers decrease waste and boost yields by adapting their actions to real-time data.

4.3 IoT for Real-time Monitoring

One of the IoT's greatest strengths is its ability to provide real-time data, allowing farmers to respond swiftly to changing conditions. IoT-driven real-time monitoring systems:

- **Environmental Monitoring:** IoT sensors continuously track variables in the environment, including temperature, humidity, and precipitation. This knowledge is crucial for forecasting weather events and streamlining agricultural operations.
- **Livestock Tracking:** Livestock using IoT-enabled ear tags and collars can have their whereabouts, health, and behavioural patterns tracked in real time. This guarantees the herd's welfare and productivity.
- **Crop Health:** Early indicators of crop stress or disease can be identified by sensors and cameras, allowing for prompt interventions to limit serious damage.

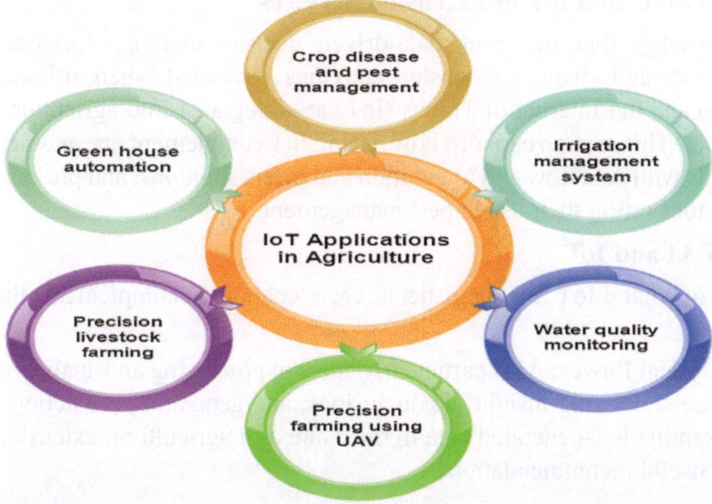

Fig. 2: Source:https://www.researchgate.net/figure/IoT-applications-in-precision-agriculture_fig2_362642925

4.4 IoT in Sustainable Farming Practices

Sustainability is a pressing concern in modern agriculture, and IoT plays a vital role in promoting environmentally friendly farming practices:

- **Resource Optimization:** IoT gadgets make it easier to manage resources like energy and water. For instance, intelligent irrigation systems save water waste by adjusting water flow based on soil moisture levels.
- **Waste Reduction:** IoT technology minimizes environmental effect by enabling precise application of fertilizers and pesticides only where necessary.
- **Eco-friendly Livestock Management:** By ensuring animals receive the proper diet, limiting the abuse of antibiotics, and lowering greenhouse gas emissions, IoT devices can improve livestock agricultural operations.

4.5 Case Studies: IoT in Livestock Management

Case Study 1: Smart Dairy Farming

IoT-enabled smart dairy farming has completely changed the industry in the Netherlands. IoT devices track the vital signs and activities of cows to check their health. Early disease identification and feeding plan optimization are made possible by this real-time data, which benefits cow health and milk production.

Case Study 2: Precision Livestock Farming

IoT gadgets are commonly used in Australia's precise livestock farming. Cattle have GPS-enabled collars that offer location information, feeding patterns, and essential health data. In addition to greater animal care, this maximizes the usage of grazing land.

5.1 Integration of AI and IoT in Extension Services

A significant synergy that improves data-driven decision-making, optimizes resource allocation, and changes extension activities is created when artificial intelligence (AI) and the Internet of Things (IoT) are integrated into agricultural extension services. This section explains how AI and IoT complement one another, outlines problems with data flow and integration and offers solutions, and presents case studies demonstrating their use in pest management.

5.2 Synergy of AI and IoT

The integration of AI and IoT is synergistic, as each technology complements the other's strengths:

- **AI's Analytical Power:** AI is particularly adept at processing and analyzing large datasets, drawing insightful conclusions, and generating predictions. AI can examine IoT-generated data in the context of agricultural extension and offer useful recommendations.

- **IoT's Data Collection:** IoT gadgets gather field data in real-time, such as weather conditions, soil moisture, and livestock health. By using this data as the basis for AI-driven analytics, suggestions can be made based on the most recent data.
- **Real-time Decision Support:** IoT devices give real-time data that is essential for making prompt decisions. Farmers can quickly adapt to changing conditions thanks to AI's processing of this data to provide customised advice.

5.3 Data Flow and Integration

Efficient data flow and integration are essential for the successful integration of AI and IoT in extension services:

- **Data Standardization:** For smooth integration, it's essential to make sure that IoT devices and AI systems use standardized data formats and protocols. This standardization enables efficient communication between various components.
- **Cloud-based Solutions:** A centralized location for storing and analyzing IoT data is offered by cloud platforms. This data may be accessed by AI algorithms, who can then analyze it and produce recommendations. This guarantees the availability and consistency of the data.
- **Interoperability:** IoT hardware from different manufacturers should be made to function together effortlessly. Devices that can communicate with one another make data integration tasks easier and give a more complete picture of farm operations.

5.4 Enhancing Extension Activities

The integration of AI and IoT enhances various extension activities, making them more effective and farmer-centric:

- **Personalized Advisory Services:** Real-time IoT data is used by AI-driven recommendation engines to provide farmers with tailored advice. For instance, the system can recommend appropriate remedies for pest control based on pest prevalence and crop health.
- **Remote Troubleshooting:** Accessing IoT-generated data and AI-driven analysis allows extension agents to remotely diagnose problems. This lessens the need for in-person visits and expedites the settlement of issues.
- **Monitoring and Alerts:** IoT sensors continuously keep an eye on things like soil moisture, humidity, and temperature. AI can send alarms and suggest remedial measures when these parameters stray from ideal levels.

5.5 Case Studies: AI and IoT Integration in Pest Control

Case Study 1: Precision Pest Control

In California, IoT and AI technologies are combined to improve grape pest control. IoT sensors gather information on temperature, humidity, and the number of pests in an area. Artificial intelligence (AI) algorithms analyze this data and offer suggestions for precise pesticide application, thereby minimizing chemical use while successfully managing pests.

Case Study 2: Real-time Disease Surveillance

AI and IoT are combined in India to create a system for monitoring crop diseases. IoT devices track ambient variables, and AI models examine this information along with previously observed disease patterns. Extension professionals are informed when a disease risk is present, allowing for pre-emptive interventions like the use of disease-resistant crop types or specialized pest treatment.

6.1 Top of Form

Challenges and Opportunities in the Integration of AI and IoT in Agricultural Extension

There are many advantages to the integration of artificial intelligence (AI) and the internet of things (IoT) in agricultural extension services, but there are also a number of issues that need to be resolved. This section examines the difficulties and opportunities presented by this integration, focusing on issues such as data security and privacy, hurdles to adoption and accessibility, capacity building and training, economic viability, sustainability, and ethical considerations.

6.2 Data Privacy and Security

Challenge: Large-scale agricultural data collection, transmission, and storage via IoT devices might give rise to worries about data security and privacy. Agencies that provide extension services to farmers must make sure that private data is safeguarded from hacker attacks and illegal access.

Opportunity: Data security risks can be reduced by using strong data encryption, safe cloud storage, and access control measures. Agricultural extension services can gain the trust of farmers and others by prioritizing data protection and abiding by regulatory regulations.

Accessibility and Adoption Barriers

Challenge: It can be difficult to guarantee everyone has access to AI and IoT technology, particularly in rural or underdeveloped areas where internet connectivity may be expensive or scarce. It's possible that many farmers lack the digital literacy needed to use these tools efficiently.

Opportunity: Governments, technology companies, and extension agencies can work together to upgrade the network, increase connectivity, and provide IoT and AI solutions at a reasonable price. All farmers can take advantage of these improvements by bridging the digital literacy gap with training programs and user-friendly interfaces.

Training and Capacity Building

Challenge: Extension workers and farmers must develop new abilities and knowledge in order to integrate AI and IoT. Resources may be limited, and there may be change opposition, for training and capacity building initiatives.

Opportunity: Extension personnel and farmers should be able to access comprehensive training programs that have been established. These courses may address data interpretation, application of AI and IoT technology, and problem-solving. Implementing training programs can be facilitated through public-private partnerships.

7. Conclusion

The adoption of AI and IoT in agricultural extension services has great promise for enhancing farmer lives, sustainability, and productivity. To make sure that the advantages are achieved fairly and responsibly, it is essential to solve the related difficulties. In order to overcome these obstacles and take advantage of the opportunities given by sophisticated technologies in agricultural extension, collaboration amongst stakeholders—including governments, extension agencies, technology providers, and farmers—will be crucial.

References

Desai, P. M. (2023). AI Integration in Indian Agricultural Extension. In S. Gupta & R. Jain (Eds.), Innovative AI Solutions for Indian Farming (pp. 123-140). Indian Agri Press.

Gupta, M. (2023). Economic Viability of Agricultural Tech in India. In R. Kumar & S. Sharma (Eds.), Economic Impacts of Farming Tech in India (pp. 175-190). New Delhi Sustainable Agri Media.

Joshi, H. R. (2023). Data Privacy and Security in Indian Agricultural Tech. In M. Khanna & R. Agarwal (Eds.), Secure Digital Agriculture in India (pp. 89-104). Indian Farm Tech Media.

Kapoor, S. R., & Reddy, V. (2023). Internet of Things (IoT) Revolutionizing Agriculture in India. In N. Verma & M. Kumar (Eds.), Smart Farming for India's Future (pp. 89-104). New Delhi Agri Connect.

Khan, A. (2023). Training and Capacity Building for Indian Farmers. In S. Bhat & M. Yadav (Eds.), Empowering Indian Farmers through Technology Training (pp. 145-160). Indian Agri Solutions.

Mehta, N. R. (2023). Challenges and Opportunities in Indian Agricultural Tech. In A. Mishra & P. Sharma (Eds.), Digital Revolution in Indian Agriculture (pp. 55-70). Mumbai Agrotech Publishing.

Patel, K. S. (2023). IoT Empowering Farmers in India. In B. Chauhan & A. Singh (Eds.), IoT Applications in Indian Agriculture (pp. 175-190). New Delhi TechBooks.

Reddy, A. S. (2023). Sustainable Agriculture and Ethics in India. In P. Choudhury & S. Malhotra (Eds.), Sustainable Farming Practices and Ethical Considerations in India (pp. 215-230). Indian Sustainable Agri Books.

Sharma, R. (2023). Accessibility and Adoption Barriers in Indian Farming Technology. In S. Verma & D. Singh (Eds.), Bridging the Digital Divide in Indian Agriculture (pp. 115-130). Hyderabad Farm Learn.

Singh, A. (2023). Digital Transformation in Indian Agriculture. In R. Sharma & S. Patel (Eds.), Advancements in Indian Agricultural Technology (pp. 45-68). Indian Agrotech Publications.

7

The Role of Women in Agriculture Breaking Gender Barriers

Mamata Nanda

Visva-Bharati University, Santiniketan, Bolpur, West-Bengal

Abstract

Empowering women in agriculture isn't just a matter of social justice; it's a strategic imperative for sustainable development, economic prosperity, and achieving food security. The chapter explores the pivotal role of market access and economic empowerment in advancing women's participation and success in the agricultural sector. Women, comprising a significant portion of the agricultural workforce, face multifaceted challenges in accessing markets, financial resources, and entrepreneurial opportunities. This chapter delves into the strategies and interventions necessary to bridge these gaps and create an enabling environment for women in agriculture. Market access emerges as a crucial aspect, emphasizing the need to provide women farmers with market information, establish linkages to value chains, and facilitate connections with buyers and markets. Empowering women as entrepreneurs involves fostering value addition, providing business training, and enhancing access to credit and financial services tailored to their needs. Additionally, policy support, gender-sensitive approaches, and collective action play instrumental roles in leveling the playing field for women in agricultural markets.

Keywords: *Women, Agriculture, Market, Empowerment, Access*

Introduction

The agricultural landscape is not just about cultivating fields; it's a narrative woven with resilience, dedication, and untold stories of women who have been the backbone of this fundamental sector for centuries. Their contributions, often overlooked or undervalued, are the bedrock of agricultural sustenance worldwide. Throughout history, women have played multifaceted roles in agriculture, nurturing crops, tending to livestock, and managing households while being instrumental in the evolution of farming practices. Despite their pivotal roles, societal norms and systemic biases have marginalized their contributions, limiting access to resources, land ownership, education, and decision-making power.

In recent decades, however, there has been a growing recognition of the indispensable role women play in agriculture. Their efforts have been a catalyst for change, driving innovation, sustainability, and community development within the agricultural sphere. The aim of this exploration is to uncover the multifaceted layers of women's involvement in agriculture, highlighting their struggles, triumphs, and the transformative potential they hold within this sector. It is a call to acknowledge, celebrate, and empower the millions of women who toil the fields, often unnoticed, yet indispensable in feeding nations. This journey into the world of women in agriculture transcends geographical boundaries. From the rice paddies of Southeast Asia tended by generations of women to the vast farmlands of Africa, where women are custodians of traditional agricultural knowledge, stories abound of their resilience, adaptability, and innovation.

This book seeks to delve into the challenges faced by women in agriculture, including unequal access to resources and the persistent gender-based discrimination prevalent in many societies. Moreover, it aims to spotlight the initiatives, successes, and innovations led by women, showcasing their potential to revolutionize farming practices, enhance food security, and drive sustainable agricultural development.

Through the lens of empowerment, this exploration will unveil the transformative impact of providing women in agriculture with equitable access to resources, education, technology, and decision-making opportunities. It will examine how such empowerment doesn't just benefit individual women but enriches entire communities and contributes to global agricultural advancements.

Historical Overview of Women's Contributions to Agriculture

Throughout history, women have been integral to agricultural practices across cultures and continents, contributing significantly to the sustenance and evolution of farming. Despite often being overlooked in historical narratives, their roles have been diverse and vital, shaping agricultural techniques, innovation, and the very foundation of food production. In ancient civilizations, women played central roles in agricultural societies. From sowing seeds to harvesting crops, their expertise was fundamental to agricultural success. In societies like ancient Egypt, Mesopotamia, and Mesoamerica, women were actively involved in cultivating and managing crops, domesticating plants, and preserving agricultural knowledge through generations. During the Middle Ages in Europe, women were central to household agriculture, responsible for managing gardens, livestock, and producing food for their families. Their knowledge of herbal medicine and plant cultivation contributed significantly to agricultural practices, although often relegated to domestic roles.

Colonial periods saw a shift in agricultural dynamics. While women continued to be essential contributors to farming, colonialism often imposed Western patriarchal structures that marginalized their roles. Nevertheless, women persisted, maintaining agricultural knowledge and practices that sustained communities. The Industrial Revolution marked a significant transition in agricultural practices, with mechanization altering the dynamics of farming. While men were often at the forefront of these changes, women continued to play crucial roles in agricultural labor, especially in tasks like planting, weeding, and harvesting. In the 20th century, particularly during World Wars I and II, women stepped into agricultural roles traditionally occupied by men, contributing substantially to food production efforts while men were at war. This period highlighted women's capability and adaptability in agricultural work, challenging societal perceptions about their roles in farming.

In developing countries, especially in regions like sub-Saharan Africa and parts of Asia and Latin America, women remain central to agriculture, constituting a significant portion of the agricultural workforce. They engage in various agricultural activities, from planting and harvesting to post-harvest processing, playing critical roles in food security and economic stability.

Despite their indispensable contributions, women often face barriers to land ownership, access to resources, and decision-making power in agriculture. Recognizing and addressing these challenges is crucial to harnessing the full potential of women in agriculture for sustainable and inclusive development in the future.

Challenges Faced by Women in the Agricultural Sector

1. **Limited Land Rights**: In many regions, women have restricted access to land ownership and control. Cultural norms, legal constraints, and inheritance laws often favor men, leaving women with limited or no land rights, impacting their ability to farm independently or access credit.
2. **Unequal Access to Resources**: Women frequently face disparities in accessing essential resources such as finance, technology, seeds, and fertilizers. Lack of access prevents them from adopting modern agricultural practices or investing in their farms, limiting productivity and income.
3. **Education and Training Barriers**: Limited education and training opportunities for women in agriculture prevent them from acquiring essential skills, knowledge about modern farming techniques, and understanding market trends, impeding their ability to innovate and compete effectively.
4. **Unpaid Care Work Burden**: Women often juggle multiple roles, balancing agricultural labor with household responsibilities and caregiving duties. The

unequal burden of unpaid care work limits their time and energy dedicated to farming activities.

5. **Limited Access to Markets and Value Chains**: Discrimination and lack of market access prevent women from selling their produce directly or accessing lucrative markets. They often encounter challenges in navigating complex value chains and negotiating fair prices for their agricultural products.
6. **Gender-Based Violence and Discrimination**: Women in agriculture frequently face gender-based violence and discrimination, both in their communities and workplaces. This creates hostile environments, impacting their confidence, safety, and ability to engage freely in agricultural activities.
7. **Under Representation in Decision-Making**: Women are often excluded from decision-making processes within agricultural institutions, cooperatives, and policy formulation. Their absence in these spaces limits their influence on policies and programs that directly affect their livelihoods.
8. **Climate Change Vulnerability**: Climate change disproportionately affects women farmers, as they have fewer resources to adapt to changing conditions. Erratic weather patterns, droughts, floods, and other climate-related challenges pose significant threats to their agricultural productivity and income.

Addressing these challenges requires comprehensive strategies that promote gender equality, including policy reforms, access to education and resources, empowering women's voices in decision-making, and fostering an enabling environment free from gender-based discrimination and violence. Empowering women in agriculture is not just about justice; it's also about enhancing food security, economic growth, and sustainable development.

Importance of Recognizing and Addressing Gender Disparities

1. **Economic Growth and Food Security**: Women make up a substantial portion of the agricultural workforce globally. When women have equal access to resources, education, and opportunities in agriculture, it significantly enhances productivity and food security. Closing gender gaps can increase agricultural output, contributing to economic growth and stability.
2. **Efficient Resource Utilization**: Women often have different agricultural knowledge and perspectives than men, which can lead to more sustainable farming practices. By involving women in decision-making and resource allocation, it's possible to leverage diverse ideas and knowledge for more efficient and environmentally friendly agricultural practices.
3. **Empowering Communities**: Women in agriculture are often key decision-makers concerning household nutrition and healthcare. When women have

control over resources and income, they tend to invest more in their families' well-being, including education and healthcare, which can positively impact entire communities.

4. **Fostering Innovation and Resilience**: Addressing gender disparities encourages innovation in agricultural practices. Women's participation brings diverse insights and approaches that foster resilience against climate change, technological advancements, and market volatility.
5. **Promoting Social Justice and Human Rights**: Gender disparities in agriculture are a matter of social justice and human rights. Ensuring equality means recognizing and addressing the systemic barriers that limit women's access to resources, land, education, and decision-making roles.
6. **Sustainable Development Goals (SDGs)**: Closing gender gaps in agriculture aligns with several of the United Nations' Sustainable Development Goals (SDGs), including zero hunger, gender equality, and decent work and economic growth. Advancing gender equality in agriculture is critical for achieving these goals.
7. **Enhancing Rural Development**: In many rural areas, agriculture is the primary livelihood. Empowering women in agriculture leads to stronger rural economies by increasing incomes, creating employment opportunities, and improving living standards.
8. **Global Food Systems**: With the world's population projected to grow, it's essential to utilize all available talent and expertise to address food production challenges. Gender equality in agriculture ensures that the sector benefits from the full spectrum of skills and experiences, driving innovation and progress.

Women Farmers Around The World

Profiles of Women Farmers from Different Regions/Countries

India - Chetna Gala Sinha: Founder of the Mann Deshi Foundation, Chetna Gala Sinha empowers rural women in India by providing financial services, entrepreneurship training, and market access. She established India's first rural co-operative bank, recognizing the potential of women as economic drivers in agriculture.

Kenya - Mary Nyambura: Mary is a smallholder farmer in Kenya, using innovative farming techniques to improve crop yields and resilience to climate change. She's part of initiatives promoting sustainable agriculture and women's leadership in farming communities.

Brazil - Raimunda Gomes da Silva: Raimunda, a farmer from Brazil, advocates for agroecology and sustainable farming practices. She champions the rights of small-scale farmers and works to preserve traditional agricultural knowledge while promoting biodiversity.

Vietnam - Nguyen Thi Hien: Nguyen is a successful entrepreneur and farmer in Vietnam. She started her own organic farm and agricultural business, demonstrating how women can lead in sustainable agriculture and value-added production.

Tanzania - Mama Anna Abdallah: Mama Anna is known for her dedication to community farming in Tanzania. She's a leader in a cooperative that empowers women through collective farming, access to markets, and agricultural education.

United States - Leah Penniman: Leah is the co-founder of Soul Fire Farm in New York, focusing on training and supporting Black, Indigenous, and people of color in sustainable farming. She's an advocate for food justice, racial equity, and land reparations.

Philippines - Erlinda T. Viva: Erlinda is a farmer in the Philippines who spearheads initiatives on organic farming and biodiversity conservation. She educates local communities about sustainable farming practices, promoting food security and environmental stewardship.

Zimbabwe - Sarudzai Chikowore: Sarudzai is a farmer and founder of a community-based organization in Zimbabwe that supports women in agriculture. She empowers women through training, access to resources, and advocating for their rights in farming communities.

Their Roles, Contributions, and Challenges in Agricultural Practices

Roles

1. **Farmers and Producers**: Women are primary producers, engaged in various farming activities such as planting, weeding, harvesting, and tending to livestock. They contribute significantly to crop cultivation and food production.
2. **Seed Keepers and Preservers of Traditional Knowledge**: Often, women are the custodians of traditional agricultural knowledge, passing down practices, seed varieties, and techniques through generations, preserving biodiversity and resilience in agriculture.
3. **Entrepreneurs and Business Leaders**: Many women farmers engage in entrepreneurial activities, establishing their own farms, agribusinesses, or cooperatives. They play pivotal roles in managing farm enterprises, value addition, and accessing markets.
4. **Community Builders and Educators**: Women in agriculture often serve as community leaders, organizing collectives, sharing knowledge, and educating others about sustainable farming practices, nutrition, and food security.

Contributions

1. **Food Production and Security**: Women contribute significantly to food production, ensuring food security for their families and communities through their work in agriculture.

2. **Preservation of Biodiversity and Sustainable Practices**: Their traditional knowledge and practices often prioritize sustainability, promoting biodiversity, soil health, and natural resource conservation.
3. **Economic Empowerment**: Women farmers' contributions to agriculture generate income and contribute to household economies, enhancing financial stability and community development.
4. **Innovation and Adaptation**: Women in agriculture often innovate and adapt farming practices, leveraging their creativity and resourcefulness to address challenges such as climate change and market fluctuations.

Challenges

1. **Access to Resources**: Limited access to land, finance, modern agricultural tools, and inputs such as seeds and fertilizers restricts women's productivity and ability to adopt modern farming methods.
2. **Education and Training**: Insufficient access to education and training hampers women's ability to adopt new technologies, improve agricultural practices, and participate effectively in decision-making.
3. **Market Access and Value Chains**: Challenges in accessing markets, fair pricing, and negotiating power limit women farmers' profitability and economic growth.
4. **Gender-Based Discrimination and Cultural Barriers**: Societal norms and gender biases often restrict women's participation in agricultural decision-making and leadership roles, perpetuating inequalities.

Gender Disparities in Agricultural Access and Rights

Land Ownership and Property Rights for Women in Agriculture

Challenges

1. **Inheritance Laws and Cultural Norms**: In many societies, inheritance laws favor male heirs, resulting in women being excluded from land ownership. Cultural norms and traditions often prioritize male ownership, denying women their right to inherit or own land.
2. **Legal Barriers and Property Rights**: Laws regarding land ownership and property rights frequently discriminate against women. Even in cases where laws exist to protect women's land rights, implementation remains a challenge due to lack of awareness or enforcement.
3. **Access to Formal Documentation**: Women often lack formal documentation proving land ownership or rights. This absence of legal documentation makes it easier for women to be displaced or denied access to land, particularly in cases of divorce or widowhood.

Impact

1. **Limited Access to Resources**: Without land ownership or secure land rights, women have restricted access to credit, agricultural inputs, and government support programs. This limits their ability to invest in farming practices and impedes agricultural productivity.
2. **Vulnerability to Displacement**: Insecure land rights make women vulnerable to land grabbing, displacement, and eviction, leading to loss of livelihoods and disruption of communities.
3. **Social and Economic Empowerment**: Land ownership is crucial for women's economic empowerment and social status. It provides them with a sense of security, autonomy, and decision-making power within their households and communities.

Solutions and Progress

1. **Legal Reforms and Policy Interventions**: Governments and policymakers can enact and enforce laws that ensure gender equality in land ownership and inheritance rights. Efforts to eliminate discriminatory practices and ensure women's access to land titles are crucial.
2. **Awareness and Capacity Building**: Empowering women with knowledge about their rights to land and property through education and awareness campaigns is vital. Providing legal literacy programs can help women understand and assert their rights effectively.
3. **Community Initiatives and Land Tenure Reforms**: Community-based initiatives and reforms that promote joint ownership, equal inheritance rights, and secure land tenure for women are essential. These initiatives can help challenge traditional norms and foster gender equality in land ownership.

Access to Resources (Land, Finance, Technology, and Education)

1 Land

- **Ownership and Rights**: Securing land ownership and tenure for women is crucial. Reforms ensuring equal rights to land and property can empower women to make long-term investments in agriculture, enhancing productivity and sustainability.
- **Access to Land**: Initiatives that facilitate access to land, such as land redistribution programs or community land schemes that prioritize women's access, can positively impact their agricultural activities.

2. Finance

- **Access to Credit**: Limited access to credit and financial services hinders women from investing in agricultural inputs, modern technologies, and expanding their farming operations. Microfinance programs tailored for women farmers can be instrumental in addressing this gap.

- **Savings and Insurance**: Encouraging women to save and providing insurance mechanisms for crop failure or natural disasters can mitigate risks associated with farming, enabling them to invest more confidently.

3. Technology

- **Digital and Agricultural Technologies**: Access to modern agricultural technologies, including improved seeds, efficient irrigation, machinery, and digital tools, can enhance productivity. Training programs that educate women on technology usage are crucial for their successful adoption.
- **Information and Extension Services**: Providing women with access to information and extension services on farming best practices, market trends, and weather forecasting via mobile technology or community programs can significantly improve their agricultural outcomes.

4. Education

- **Formal Education**: Increasing educational opportunities for girls and women in rural areas ensures they have the knowledge and skills needed for better agricultural practices, financial management, and decision-making.
- **Training and Capacity Building**: Targeted training programs in agriculture, business management, and leadership empower women to make informed decisions, manage their farms efficiently, and engage in broader agricultural initiatives.

Innovations and Technologies for Women in Agriculture

Accessible Farming Technologies

- **Labor-Saving Tools**: Developing and providing tools specifically designed to reduce the physical burden of agricultural tasks, such as ergonomic hand tools or mechanized equipment suitable for women, can improve efficiency.
- **Mobile Applications**: Creating user-friendly mobile apps that offer agricultural information, market prices, weather updates, and access to extension services can empower women with valuable knowledge and resources.

2. Sustainable Agricultural Practices

- **Agroecology and Organic Farming**: Promoting agroecological approaches and organic farming methods can benefit women farmers by reducing input costs, preserving soil fertility, and promoting healthier ecosystems.
- **Climate-Resilient Technologies**: Introducing climate-resilient crop varieties, drought-resistant seeds, and innovative irrigation systems helps women farmers adapt to climate change and mitigate risks associated with unpredictable weather patterns.

3. Financial Inclusion and Technology

- **Mobile Banking and Digital Payments**: Facilitating mobile banking services and digital payment systems enables women to access financial services conveniently, conduct transactions, and save money securely.
- **Fintech Solutions**: Developing fintech solutions tailored for women farmers, such as microfinance apps or peer-to-peer lending platforms, can improve access to credit and financial resources.

4. Education and Training Programs

- **E-Learning Platforms**: Creating online educational platforms with courses on agricultural best practices, financial management, and entrepreneurship allows women to access training and knowledge remotely.
- **Tech-Enabled Extension Services**: Using technology to provide extension services, virtual workshops, and expert consultations helps women farmers stay updated on new techniques and innovations.

5. Gender-Inclusive Technology Design

- **Consultative Approach**: Engaging women farmers in the design and development of agricultural technologies ensures that innovations meet their specific needs, preferences, and cultural contexts.
- **User-Centered Design**: Designing technologies with user-friendly interfaces and considering the physical capabilities and cultural nuances of women farmers enhances the adoption and effectiveness of these innovations.

Market Access And Economic Opportunities For Women

1. Access to Markets

- **Market Information**: Providing women with access to market information, trends, and pricing helps them make informed decisions about what and when to sell, ensuring better returns for their produce.
- **Market Linkages and Value Chains**: Facilitating connections between women farmers and markets, including linking them with buyers, processors, retailers, or cooperatives, enhances their access to broader markets.

2. Entrepreneurship and Value Addition

- **Value-Added Products**: Supporting women in adding value to their agricultural produce through processing, packaging, and branding can increase the profitability of their goods.
- **Business Training and Development**: Equipping women with entrepreneurship skills, financial literacy, and business management training enables them to run successful agricultural enterprises.

3. Financial Inclusion

- **Access to Credit and Financial Services**: Improving access to credit, savings, and insurance products tailored for women farmers helps them invest in their farms, manage risks, and expand their businesses.
- **Microfinance and Savings Groups**: Establishing microfinance programs and women-led savings and lending groups empowers women economically and enhances their financial independence.

4. Policy Support and Gender-Sensitive Approaches

- **Gender-Responsive Policies**: Advocating for policies that address gender inequalities in access to markets, land rights, and financial services is crucial for creating an enabling environment for women in agriculture.
- **Inclusive Value Chain Development**: Ensuring that value chain development programs prioritize women's participation, benefit sharing, and capacity-building supports their integration into markets.

5. Collective Action and Networking

- **Cooperatives and Collectives**: Encouraging women to form cooperatives or collectives allows them to collectively access markets, negotiate better prices, and share resources and knowledge.
- **Networking and Partnerships**: Facilitating networking opportunities and partnerships with other stakeholders, including government bodies, NGOs, and private sector entities, opens doors to market access and support systems.

Conclusion

The vital role of women in agriculture transcends stereotypes and challenges traditional gender norms. Their immense contributions drive innovation, sustainability, and resilience within the agricultural sector. As women continue to break barriers, their empowerment not only enhances food security but also fosters economic growth and social progress. Recognizing and supporting their efforts through equal access to resources, education, and leadership opportunities is not just a matter of equality but a strategic investment in a more prosperous and equitable future for the agricultural landscape and beyond. Empowering women in agriculture is not merely a choice; it's a necessity for a thriving global community.

References

Ahammad, I., & Moudud-Ul-Huq, S. (2013). Women entrepreneurship development In Bangladesh challenges and prospects. *International Journal of Innovative Research and Development*, 2(7), 41-48. Retrieved from https://www.researchgate.net/publication/281115595

Ahmed, F., Siwar, C., Idris, N. A. H., & Begum, R. A. (2011). Impact of Gramen Bank microcredit program on changing livelihood status of the rural women in Panchagarh district of Bangladesh. *American Journal of Applied Sciences*, 8(10), 973–978. Retrieved from https://thescipub.com/abstract/ajassp.2011.973.978

Ali, I., & Hatta, Z. A. (2012). Women's empowerment or disempowerment through microfinance: Evidence from Bangladesh. *Asian Social Work and Policy Review*, 6(2), 111–121. Retrieved from https://onlinelibrary.wiley.com/doi/10.1111/j.1753-1411.2012.00066.x

Alkire, S., Meinzen-Dick, R., Peterman, A., Quisumbing, A., Seymour, G., & Vaz, A. (2013). The women's empowerment in agriculture index. *World Development,* 5(2), 71–91. Retrieved from https://www.ophi.org.uk/wp-content/uploads/ophi-wp-58.pdf

Awasthi, N., Sahu, A., Singh, A. K., & Tripathi, M. N. (2020). Constraints in Empowerment of Rural Women in District Kanpur Dehat U.P. *Indian Journal of Extension Education*, 56(3), 37–40. Retrieved from https://epubs.icar.org.in/index.php/IJEE/article/view/107002

Chowdhury, S. S., & Chowdhury, S. A. (2011). Microfinance and women empowerment: A panel data analysis using evidence from rural Bangladesh. *International Journal of Economics & Finance*, 3(5),86–96. Retrieved from https://www.ccsenet.org/journal/index.php/ijef/article/view/12321

Jadoun, Y. (2021). Gender Mainstreaming through Livestock Entrepreneurship. *Indian Journal of Extension Education*, 55(2), 61–69. Retrieved from https://epubs.icar.org.in/index.php/IJEE/article/view/109201

8

Empowering Women and Youth in Agriculture: Bridging Gender Disparities and Fostering Innovation for Sustainability

[1]Maitreyee Tripathy, [2]Rajiv Nayan Das and [3]Subhashree Mishra

[1]Odisha University of Agriculture & Technology, Bhubaneswar, Odisha
[2]MGN Fellow, IIM Bangalore, Karnataka
[3]IAS, SOA, Bhubaneswar, Odisha

Abstract

This chapter highlights the significant contributions made by Indian women and young people to the agricultural industry, with an emphasis on resolving persistent gender imbalances. It emphasizes the necessity of redressing these discrepancies in order to foster a more equitable and sustainable agricultural landscape through an examination of recent statistical data. It explores numerous facets, including education, resource accessibility, leadership representation, and agricultural innovation. By doing this, it presents a thorough viewpoint on the potential for empowering women and young people to advance agricultural innovation and sustainability. Its investigation highlights the severe gender differences that still exist in agricultural leadership roles, education, resource access, and land ownership. The examination of the young population's migratory patterns from rural to urban areas is also crucial. Young Indians are emerging as agripreneurship leaders throughout this migration, adopting sustainable farming methods and developing cutting-edge technical advancements. This chapter essentially emphasizes the necessity of developing gender-responsive policies, supporting youth-driven initiatives, and closing the digital divide in rural areas. These steps are essential to promoting an inclusive, creative, and environmentally sound agricultural sector in India, assuring long-term food security and economic development.

Keywords: *Agricultural Empowerment, Gender Equity, Youth Engagement, Sustainable Farming*

Introduction

The foundation of human civilization has traditionally been agriculture, which offers sustenance, economic security, and a strong bond with the land. Nevertheless, although playing a crucial role, the global agricultural sector faces many difficulties, including resource shortages and climate change as well as a fast-expanding population. The empowerment of women and young people in agriculture stands out as a critical answer in this situation, driving not only agricultural sustainability but also promoting social and economic advancement. In agriculture, empowerment refers to the fair inclusion and active involvement of women and young people in all facets of the industry, including leadership and decision-making as well as production and distribution. It admits that despite these groups' enormous latent potential, they have been ignored and underutilized for far too long. By unlocking the contributions of women and youth, we can build resilient agricultural systems that address contemporary challenges while ensuring a prosperous and sustainable future for all.

1.1 Background

The Significance of Agriculture in India's Economy

India's economy has always been based on agriculture, which supports a large amount of the country's people and generates a considerable portion of its GDP. Over 50% of the workforce is employed in agriculture, which generates around 16% of India's overall GDP, according to the Economic Survey 2020-2021. This industry not only supports rural areas, but it also contributes significantly to the stability and food security of the entire country.

The Gender Gap in Agriculture

Despite the vital significance that agriculture plays in India, there is an obvious gender imbalance in this industry. Women, who make up a sizable portion of the agricultural workforce, frequently experience unfairness in terms of their ability to access resources and make decisions. According to the National Sample Survey (NSS) 2019-2020, just 13.9% of rural women and 87.1% of rural males own land collectively within the agricultural labor force. These inequalities cover a variety of topics, including involvement in leadership positions within agricultural organizations, access to loans, and agricultural inputs.

Youth Involvement in Agriculture

Another important feature of the dynamics of the sector is the involvement of young people in agriculture. The World Bank estimates that 34.8% of India's population is under the age of 34 (World Bank, 2020). However, there has been a clear trend of young people from rural areas moving to cities in quest of better job possibilities. The number of rural men working in agriculture has been progressively falling over time, according to the NSS 2017–2018, showing a move away from conventional agricultural techniques.

1.2 Purpose of the Chapter

Addressing Gender Disparities

This chapter's main goal is to overcome the gender gaps that still exist in India's agriculture sector. From unequal land ownership to restricted access to resources and leadership positions, these discrepancies take many different forms. According to statistics, only 56.8% of rural women between the ages of 15 and 49 have finished at least five years of education (NSS 2017–2018). We want to study the effects of these inequities as well as the measures and policies that have been put in place to address them.

Empowering Youth

This chapter focuses on the empowerment of Indian youth in agriculture as well as gender inequities. Rural-to-urban migration is a serious problem, but there are youth-led programs and agricultural ventures that show hope for the industry. If appropriately employed in worthwhile pursuits like agriculture, India's youth population might possibly represent a demographic dividend, according to the World Bank. We'll look at how youth involvement could energize the agriculture industry.

Promoting Innovation for Sustainability

The final point made in this chapter is how crucial it is to foster innovation if agriculture is to remain sustainable. For the preservation of the ecosystem and long-term food security, sustainable farming methods are crucial. The Paramparagat Krishi Vikas Yojana (PKVY) and other programs work to promote sustainable farming methods and organic farming. We emphasize the way forward for a more sustainable and inclusive agricultural ecosystem by presenting youth-driven solutions and gender-responsive policy.

2. Gender Disparities in Agriculture

2.1 Access to Land and Property Rights

Statistical Data on Land Ownership by Gender

India's gender disparity in land ownership is a serious problem. Only 13.9% of the operating holdings in the country are owned by rural women, while 87.1% are controlled by rural men, according to the National Sample Survey (NSS) 2019-2020. These figures demonstrate a significant gender gap in land ownership.

Implications of Unequal Land Distribution

For rural women, unequal land allocation has significant ramifications. Land ownership promotes social empowerment in addition to economic security. It gives people control over agricultural activity, access to credit, and the chance to take part in government initiatives. Rural women may become financially dependent, have little say in household decisions, and have less access to resources as a result of the unequal distribution of land.

Policies and Initiatives Addressing Land Rights

In order to remedy these inequities, a number of policies and programs have been put into place. The Mahila Kisan Sashaktikaran Pariyojana (MKSP), which aims to empower women in agriculture, is one noteworthy effort. MKSP gives women farmers the tools and resources they need to proactively establish their land rights, gain access to resources, and engage in agricultural operations. The government has also implemented reforms to strengthen the documentation and land titling procedures, making it simpler for women to establish land ownership.

2.2 Access to Agricultural Inputs and Resources

Disparities in Access to Seeds, Fertilizers, and Machinery

There is still a gender gap in access to basic agricultural inputs including high-quality seeds, fertilizer, and equipment. The National Bank for Agriculture and Rural Development's (NABARD) records show that women farmers have limited access to financing, which has an impact on their ability to buy inputs. Crop yields, productivity, and overall profitability of women-led agricultural enterprises are all impacted by this access divide.

Women's Role in Resource Management

Despite differences, women are essential to household resource management. They frequently take on duties connected to post-harvest processing, animal care, and water management. Their efforts are, however, usually overlooked and underappreciated. This emphasizes how essential it is to give women equal access to resources as well as to recognize and value their contributions to resource management.

Government Schemes Promoting Equal Access

To encourage fair access to agricultural resources and inputs, the Indian government has developed a number of programs and initiatives. There are provisions in the Rashtriya Krishi Vikas Yojana (RKVY) and the National Mission on Agriculture Extension and Technology (NMAET) to improve women's access to contemporary farming inputs and technologies. Additionally, the establishment of women's self-help organizations and cooperatives has encouraged resource sharing and collective purchase, enabling women to make knowledgeable decisions about agricultural inputs.

2.3 Education and Training

Literacy Rates Among Female Farmers

In India, female farmers' literacy rates have increased over time, yet discrepancies still exist. The overall literacy rate for women in rural regions was 55.1% in 2011, according to the Census of India, showing that a sizable proportion of rural women lack basic literacy abilities. Their capacity to obtain information, adopt contemporary farming methods, and make wise judgments are all impacted by this literacy divide.

Importance of Education for Agricultural Practices

An important factor in improving agricultural practices is education. It provides farmers with the information and abilities necessary for using technology, managing resources effectively, and engaging in sustainable farming. Farmers with more education are more likely to adopt cutting-edge practices, increasing crop yields and improving their standard of living.

Initiatives to Enhance Female Agricultural Education

Several programs have been launched to improve female agriculture education. One such initiative is the National Agriculture Higher Education Project (NAHEP), which aims to raise the standard of agricultural education and improve graduates' skills in agricultural techniques, especially those of women. Additionally, training and awareness initiatives aimed at enhancing the abilities of women in agriculture are carried out by non-governmental organizations (NGOs) and self-help groups.

2.4 Gender-Based Income Disparities

Wage Gaps in Agricultural Labor

Income differences based on gender still exist in the agricultural workforce. For similar agricultural labour, women frequently make less money than men do. Women in South Asia who work in agriculture make, on average, 70% of what males do, according to data from the International Labor Organization (ILO). Factors including unequal access to resources, weak negotiating power, and discrimination in the job market all have an impact on this wage disparity.

Women's Contribution to the Agricultural Workforce

The agricultural workforce significantly benefits from the contributions of women. They actively participate in a variety of farming tasks, including as planting, weeding, harvesting, and processing after the harvest. Their efforts are crucial to the production of food and the health of the agricultural industry as a whole.

Strategies for Income Equality

Strategies should emphasize equal compensation for equal labor and providing opportunity for women in higher-paying positions in agriculture in order to address income disparity. The wage gap can be reduced with the use of wage-setting procedures and labor laws that are gender-sensitive. Furthermore, increasing women's access to resources, training, and finance can boost their productivity and income-generating capacity.

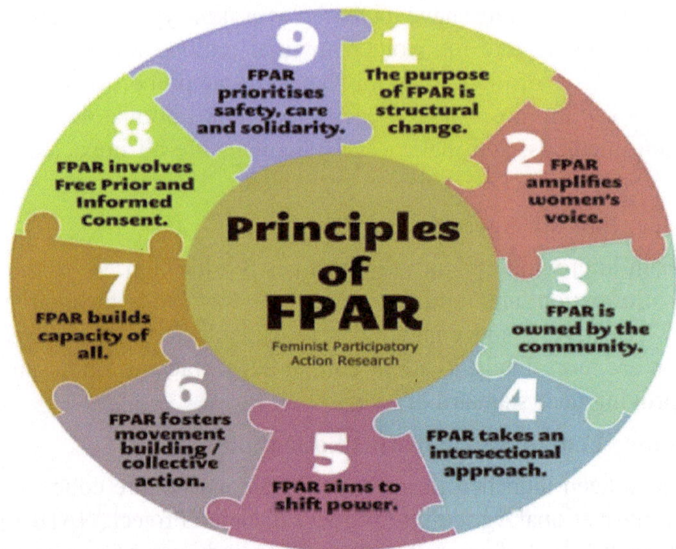

Fig. 1: Principles of FPAR (*Source*).

2.5 Leadership and Decision-Making

Representation of Women in Agricultural Leadership Roles

Women continue to be underrepresented in positions of leadership in the agriculture industry. In positions of power, particularly those in self-help organizations, farming associations, and agricultural cooperatives, women are underrepresented. Only 15% of agricultural landowners in India are women, according to the World Bank, and female involvement in decision-making is frequently low.

The Need for Women's Participation in Decision-Making

For the creation of agricultural policies and practices that are gender-responsive, women must actively participate in decision-making processes. Women's particular objectives and views can result in more inclusive and successful tactics. Making decisions that are gender-sensitive can help women in agriculture overcome unique obstacles and advance their empowerment.

Success Stories of Female Leaders in Agriculture

Inspiring success stories of female leaders in agriculture exist despite the obstacles. Women who have broken down barriers and shown that they can lead and affect positive change in rural communities include Chhavi Rajawat, who became India's first woman sarpanch (village head) with an MBA. Such tales serve as inspiration for ambitious female agricultural leaders.

3. The Role of Indian Youth in Agriculture

3.1 Youth Migration to Urban Areas

Causes and Consequences of Rural-to-Urban Migration

Numerous causes, such as the dearth of employment possibilities in rural areas, the attractiveness of metropolitan lifestyles, and hopes for improved economic prospects, contribute to the rural-to-urban movement of Indian youth. This migration has a wide range of effects. It lessens the strain on rural agricultural labor markets, but it may also result in a shortage of trained farm employees, which would lower agricultural productivity. It also puts a burden on urban services and infrastructure, posing additional difficulties for metropolitan regions.

Challenges Faced by Rural Youth

Rural kids confront a number of difficulties, including limited access to high-quality education and agricultural career training. This restricts their ability to take part in agricultural endeavors and contemporary farming techniques. Their capacity to invest in agricultural ventures may also be hampered by a lack of access to financing and financial services. Additionally, the digital gap in rural communities worsens their isolation from agricultural technology breakthroughs.

3.2 Youth Engagement in Agripreneurship

Emerging Trends in Agripreneurship

The word "agripreneurship," which mixes agriculture and entrepreneurship, is becoming more popular among young people in India. Young people are increasingly investigating novel and commercially focused ways to agriculture. This includes businesses like organic farming, farm-to-table programs, and startup agri-tech companies. These initiatives support sustainable farming methods while also fostering economic prosperity.

Success Stories of Young Agripreneurs

Young agripreneurs who have successfully turned their love of agriculture into successful businesses are numerous. Sangeeta Taluja, the creator of EarthCraft Herbals, for instance, shifted to organic farming and herb growing to give rural women sustainable incomes. Such success tales show how youth-led agribusinesses have the power to spur agricultural innovation and generate job opportunities.

Government Support for Youth in Agriculture

The Indian government has started a number of measures to boost young involvement in agriculture because it understands how important it is. The Atmanirbhar Bharat Abhiyan has measures for fostering agripreneurship and allowing young farmers' and entrepreneurs' access to loans. For rural youth interested in agribusiness, programs like the National Rural Livelihoods Mission (DAY-NRLM) offer training and financial assistance.

3.3 Technology Adoption and Innovation

The Digital Divide in Rural Areas

India's rural areas frequently experience a digital gap due to their restricted access to technical tools and the internet. This gap makes it difficult for young people in rural areas to take advantage of agricultural technology improvements like precision farming, data analytics, and market information access. Additionally, it restricts their access to recent agricultural trends.

Youth-Led Technological Innovations

In spite of the digital divide, many young people in rural areas have taken the initiative to create tech-based agricultural solutions. For example, real-time weather forecasts are provided by mobile applications, which are also used to connect farmers to markets and communicate agricultural information. Crop yields are rising as a result of these advancements, which also improve farming techniques.

Bridging the Technology Gap

To fully realize the promise of youth-led innovation, it is imperative to close the technology divide in rural areas. Rural areas' connectivity and digital infrastructure are being improved by programs like the Digital India initiative. Furthermore, vocational training programs must to give rural kids the abilities they need to use technology in agriculture. Partnerships between the public and commercial sectors can be very helpful in making sure that technical developments reach the general public.

4. Driving Agricultural Innovation and Sustainability

4.1 Gender-Responsive Agricultural Policies

Policy Recommendations for Gender-Inclusive Agriculture

To promote gender equality in agriculture, it is essential to adopt and implement gender-responsive agricultural policies. These policies should focus on several key areas:

- **Land Rights:** providing women with clear legal protections, open access to land registration and documentation processes, and equal rights to land ownership and tenure.
- **Access to Resources:** Equal access to loans, extension services, and agricultural inputs like seeds, fertilizer, and machinery is made possible by targeted financial incentives and initiatives that create capacity.
- **Education and Training:** Encouraging women to pursue careers in agriculture to give them the information and skills needed for contemporary farming and agribusiness.
- **Leadership and Decision-Making:** Encouraging women to take on leadership positions within agricultural cooperatives and organizations, as

well as to participate in policy- and decision-making processes on a local and national level.

- **Data Collection and Analysis:** Enhancing the gathering and analysis of data that is gender-disaggregated to track and assess how policies and actions are affecting women in agriculture.
- **Case Studies of Successful Gender-Responsive Policies:** A number of nations and areas have successfully developed agricultural strategies that take gender into account. For instance, the property Tenure Regularization Program in Rwanda has greatly increased the rights of women to own property, improving their economic empowerment and household decision-making. The Mahila Kisan Sashaktikaran Pariyojana (MKSP) in India has also been successful in empowering women via education, resource access, and group effort.

4.2 Youth-Driven Sustainable Practices

Youth-Led Sustainable Farming Techniques

Indian youth are leading the way in creating and implementing sustainable farming practices. They are embracing techniques like permaculture, organic farming, and zero-budget natural farming (ZBNF). These techniques prioritize protecting the environment, utilize less pesticides, and improve soil health. Youth-led programs like "Organic Farming Startups" and "Green Youth Movement" are educating their peers about sustainable agriculture.

Promoting Eco-Friendly Agriculture Among Youth

To encourage eco-friendly agriculture among youth, it is crucial to:

- **Provide Training:** Provide specialist training courses and workshops with an emphasis on agroecology, organic farming, and sustainable farming methods.
- **Financial Support:** Give people access to inexpensive, environmentally friendly inputs and financial incentives for adopting sustainable behaviors.
- **Awareness Campaigns:** Start public awareness campaigns stressing the advantages of sustainable farming for the environment and its contribution to the preservation of natural resources.

4.3 Empowering Women and Youth Through Training

Skill Development Programs for Women and Youth

Skill development programs tailored to the needs of women and youth are essential for enhancing their capacities for innovation and sustainability in agriculture. These programs should encompass:

- **Technical Skills:** Training in modern farming techniques, resource management, and the use of technology for agriculture.

- **Financial Literacy:** Education on financial management, budgeting, and accessing credit and loans.
- **Entrepreneurship Skills:** Training in agribusiness management, marketing, and value chain development.

Enhancing Their Capacity for Innovation and Sustainability

Women's and youth's empowerment through training not only provides them with necessary skills but also promotes an innovative and sustainable culture. These people can help ensure the agricultural industry's long-term viability by giving them the resources and information they need to adjust to shifting market conditions and farming practices.

5. Conclusion

5.1 Recapitulation of Key Points

In this chapter, we have explored the critical issues surrounding gender disparities in agriculture and the pivotal role played by Indian youth in driving agricultural innovation and sustainability. The key points discussed include:

- **Gender Disparities in Agriculture:** We looked at the enormous gender gaps that still exist in land ownership, resource access, education, pay, and leadership positions in agriculture. The full potential of women in the agriculture sector is hampered by these inequities.
- **The Pivotal Role of Indian Youth:** We emphasized the significance of empowering and involving Indian youth in agriculture, despite the difficulties brought on by migration from rural to urban areas. Young people are important change agents because they offer new perspectives, creativity, and vigor to the industry.
- **Driving Innovation and Sustainability:** We looked at the role that youth-led sustainable practices, gender-responsive policies, and training programs can play in promoting agricultural innovation and sustainability. The development of an agricultural ecosystem that is more inclusive and environmentally sensitive depends on these initiatives.

5.2 Implications and Future Outlook

The Importance of Continued Efforts to Empower Women

In addition to being important for achieving gender equality, empowering women in agriculture is also crucial for the sector's overall growth. We must constantly improve and broaden the policies and programs that address gender gaps, such as those that promote equitable land allocation, access to resources, education, and leadership opportunities. It is essential for women to actively participate in decision-making processes in order to create policies that address their unique requirements.

Leveraging Youth for Agricultural Transformation

India's youth population offers a large opportunity for agricultural development. It is crucial to keep encouraging young people to engage in agribusiness, environmentally friendly farming methods, and technology innovation in order to fully realize this potential. The goal of public assistance and private sector participation should be to foster an environment that promotes youth employment in agriculture as a feasible and alluring career path.

Achieving Sustainable Agriculture Through Inclusivity

Inclusion is key to agricultural sustainability. We can create a more resilient and ecologically sustainable agriculture economy by empowering women and young people. It is important to promote and scale up sustainable techniques including organic farming, precision agriculture, and prudent resource management. The consideration of all stakeholders' interests in the formation of decisions and policies guarantees that they are more sustainable and equitable.

References

Godden, N.J.; Macnish, P.; Chakma, T.; Naidu, K. Feminist participatory action research as a tool for climate justice. Gend. Dev. 2020, 28, 593–615.

International Labour Organization (ILO). (2021). Gender and Rural Employment in India: A Review of Current Trends and Policy Issues. ILO Report.

Ministry of Agriculture & Farmers Welfare, Government of India. (2021). Rashtriya Krishi Vikas Yojana (RKVY).

Ministry of Finance, Government of India. (2020). Atmanirbhar Bharat Abhiyan.

Ministry of Finance, Government of India. (2021). Economic Survey 2020-2021.

Ministry of Rural Development, Government of India. (2021). Mahila Kisan Sashaktikaran Pariyojana (MKSP).

Ministry of Statistics and Programme Implementation, Government of India. (2018). National Sample Survey (NSS) 2017-2018.

Ministry of Statistics and Programme Implementation, Government of India. (2020). National Sample Survey (NSS) 2019-2020.

National Bank for Agriculture and Rural Development (NABARD). (2021). Status of Microfinance in India 2020-21. NABARD Report.

Office of the Registrar General & Census Commissioner, India. (2011). Provisional Population Totals. Census of India 2011.

World Bank. (2020). India - Systematic Country Diagnostic: Inclusion and Jobs. World Bank Report.

9

Biodynamic Farming Bridging Spirituality and Sustainable Agriculture

[1]S.P. Monalisa, [2]Spandit Kar and [3]Sona Saloni Parida

[1]Assistant professor, Seed Science and Technology, Faculty of Agricultural Sciences, SOADU, Bhubaneswar, Odisha
[2]Seed Science and Technology, Faculty of Agricultural Sciences, SOA Bhubaneswar, Odisha
[3]Seed Science and Technology, Faculty of AgriculturalSciences, SOA Bhubaneswar, Odisha

ABSTRACT:

In the realm of modern agriculture, Bio Dynamic Farming emerges as a profound synthesis of ancient wisdom and contemporary sustainability practices. This chapter delves into the intricate tapestry of Bio Dynamic Farming, weaving together spirituality and sustainable agriculture. Drawing inspiration from Rudolf Steiner's anthroposophy, this holistic approach transcends the mere cultivation of crops, aiming to harmonize the spiritual, ecological, and cosmic forces at play in the farming ecosystem.

Keywords: *Biodynamic Farming, Sustainable Agriculture, Spiritual Ecology, Organic Farming Practices, Holistic Farm Management*

Introduction

The dawn of the 21st century brings with it unprecedented challenges for agriculture - challenges that demand a departure from conventional practices and a harmonious integration of spirituality and sustainable methodologies. In this pursuit, Bio Dynamic Farming emerges as a beacon, guiding farmers to cultivate not only crops but also a deeper understanding of the spiritual dimensions intertwined with the earth's rhythms. Rooted in the visionary teachings of Rudolf Steiner and his anthroposophical principles, Bio Dynamic Farming transcends the mechanistic view of agriculture, offering a holistic paradigm where spirituality and sustainable agriculture dance in unison.

Anthroposophy: A Spiritual Science for the Earth

At the heart of Bio Dynamic Farming lies anthroposophy, a spiritual science developed by Rudolf Steiner in the early 20th century. Steiner's vision extended beyond the physical realm, encompassing the spiritual dimensions that influence all aspects of life, including agriculture. Anthroposophy posits that the earth is not merely a resource to exploit but a living, spiritual organism. It emphasizes the interconnectedness of the material and spiritual worlds, encouraging practitioners to cultivate an awareness that goes beyond the tangible aspects of farming.

Steiner's lectures, particularly those delivered in 1924 to a group of farmers concerned about the declining quality of their crops, laid the foundation for Bio Dynamic Farming. In these lectures, he expounded upon the need to consider the farm as a self-sustaining organism, with the farmer as its steward, nurturing not only the soil but also the spiritual forces at play. Thus, Bio Dynamic Farming emerged as a transformative approach that blended spiritual insights with practical agricultural techniques.

The Living Soil: Nurturing Vitality Through Biodynamic Preparations

A cornerstone of Bio Dynamic Farming is the recognition of soil as a living entity. Conventional agriculture often views soil merely as a medium to anchor roots and provide nutrients. In contrast, Biodynamic Farming perceives the soil as a dynamic, living organism with its own rhythms and energies. Practitioners believe that fostering the vitality of the soil is paramount for cultivating healthy and resilient crops.Biodynamic preparations, a set of specially formulated substances, are a testament to this belief. These preparations, including horn manure and horn silica, are applied in minute quantities to enhance the life forces within the soil. They act as conduits, channelling cosmic energies into the earth, aligning the farm with larger celestial rhythms. In the dance between the ethereal and the earthly, biodynamic preparations serve as the choreographers, orchestrating a symphony of life in the soil.

Cosmic Rhythms: Planting with the Stars and the Moon

One of the distinctive features of Bio Dynamic Farming is its embrace of cosmic influences on agricultural activities. While this might seem esoteric to some, practitioners consider the lunar and celestial cycles as potent forces shaping the life on the farm. The planting and harvesting times are not arbitrary but meticulously aligned with these cosmic rhythms. Observing the phases of the moon and the positions of celestial bodies becomes an integral aspect of Bio Dynamic Farming. Planting decisions are made in harmony with these cosmic forces, seeking to optimize the energy flow within the plants. The moon, acting as a celestial guide, influences water movement in plants and soil, impacting germination and growth.

This cosmic dance is not just a mystical ritual; it is a practical manifestation of aligning agricultural activities with the larger cosmic symphony.

Sustainability Woven into Spirituality: The Practical Aspects of Bio Dynamic Farming

Amidst the ethereal tapestry of spirituality, Bio Dynamic Farming stands firmly on the ground of sustainable agriculture. The practices embedded in this approach are not mere rituals; they are pragmatic steps towards nurturing the earth's resources responsibly. Crop rotation, cover cropping, and composting are integral components of Bio Dynamic Farming, contributing to soil health and biodiversity. Crop rotation disrupts pest and disease cycles, promoting a balanced ecosystem without reliance on synthetic chemicals. Cover cropping enriches the soil with organic matter and acts as a natural weed suppressant. Composting, another fundamental practice, recycles organic waste, returning nutrients to the soil and reducing the environmental impact of farming.

In the fusion of spirituality and sustainability, Bio Dynamic Farming offers a comprehensive model that transcends the dichotomy between the spiritual and the practical. It stands as a testament to the notion that agriculture can be a harmonious coexistence of the mystical and the pragmatic, where the farm becomes a living testament to the interconnectedness of all life forms.

Challenges on the Path and the Promise of Collaboration

While the principles of Bio Dynamic Farming resonate with a growing number of individuals, it is not without its challenges. Scepticism within the scientific community, logistical difficulties in implementing certain practices, and the need for broader acceptance pose formidable hurdles. The chapter delves into these challenges, offering insights into potential solutions and avenues for collaboration between scientific rigor and spiritual intuition.

Cultivating A Spiritual Ecology: A Deeper Dive into Biodynamic Farming Practices

Having established the foundations of Bio Dynamic Farming in the interplay between spirituality and sustainability, this chapter now delves deeper into the intricate practices that define this transformative approach. From cosmic rhythms to biodynamic preparations, each element plays a crucial role in weaving the ethereal and the earthly into a tapestry of agricultural harmony.

Cosmic Rhythms in Action: A Lunar Ballet for Planting

In the ballet of the cosmos, Bio Dynamic Farming choreographs its planting rituals with the precision of a cosmic dance. Lunar cycles, in particular, become a guiding force for farmers practicing this approach. The waxing and waning phases of the moon influence various aspects of plant growth, and practitioners align their activities accordingly. The lunar calendar becomes a farmer's almanac, guiding decisions on when to sow, transplant, and harvest. Planting during the waxing moon is believed to enhance above-ground growth, while activities during the waning moon focus on root development. This nuanced approach to timing is not mere superstition; it reflects a profound understanding of the subtle energies at play in the agricultural realm. The moon, acting as a celestial conductor, directs the symphony of growth on the farm.

Biodynamic Preparations: Elixirs of Cosmic Vitality

At the heart of Bio Dynamic Farming's spiritual alchemy are the biodynamic preparations, mystical elixirs crafted to channel cosmic forces into the soil. Horn manure (preparation 500) and horn silica (preparation 501) are among the most renowned. The former, prepared by burying cow horns filled with manure over the winter, enhances soil structure and microbial activity. The latter, made from crushed quartz buried in a cow horn over the summer, stimulates photosynthesis and strengthens the plant's connection to the cosmos.

Applying these preparations in infinitesimally small amounts might seem esoteric, but practitioners attest to their transformative effects. It's not merely about the physical substances applied to the land; it's about awakening the dormant forces within the soil. The farm, in this paradigm, becomes a canvas for the interplay of earthly and cosmic energies, each biodynamic preparation serving as a brushstroke in a masterpiece painted by nature.

Spiritual Ecology in Crop Rotation

Crop rotation, a time-honoured agricultural practice, takes on a spiritual dimension in Bio Dynamic Farming. Beyond the pragmatic benefits of pest and disease control, practitioners see it as a dance of energies. Different crops are believed to have distinct spiritual qualities, and rotating them creates a dynamic exchange of forces within the soil.

In this spiritual ecology, each crop contributes its unique energy to the farm organism. Legumes, with their nitrogen-fixing abilities, are seen as embodying a supportive and harmonizing force. Cereals, with their upward growth, channel cosmic forces into the earth. Root crops, delving deep, bring a grounding energy. By orchestrating this dance of energies, farmers seek not only a bountiful harvest but also a balanced and spiritually enriched agricultural landscape.

Cover Cropping: The Green Mantle of the Earth

Cover cropping, another practice within Bio Dynamic Farming, serves both practical and spiritual purposes. From a sustainability standpoint, cover crops prevent soil erosion, suppress weeds, and add organic matter to the soil. But beyond these ecological benefits, they are seen as the green mantle, a protective and nourishing cloak for the earth. Legumes, such as clover and vetch, are often chosen for cover cropping due to their nitrogen-fixing abilities. As these plants flourish, they weave a green tapestry across the fields, contributing not only to soil health but also symbolizing the farm's connection to the natural cycles of growth and renewal. The cover crop becomes a living prayer, a testament to the commitment of the farmer to nurture the land in harmony with the spiritual currents flowing through nature.

Composting: From Waste to Cosmic Renewal

In the cycle of life and death, composting stands as a sacred act in Bio Dynamic Farming. Organic waste, once considered refuse, transforms into a cosmic elixir for the soil. Practitioners see compost not just as a source of nutrients but as a medium for recycling and renewing the energies within the farm. The compost heap, akin to an alchemical cauldron, blends diverse organic materials into a potent mixture. This mixture, enriched with cosmic forces through the biodynamic preparations, becomes a nourishing elixir for the soil. Composting is not just a practical waste management strategy; it is a spiritual communion with the cycles of life, a conscious effort to participate in the cosmic dance of creation and renewal.

Challenges and Collaborations: Bridging the Spiritual and the Scientific

As practitioners delve into the depths of Bio Dynamic Farming, challenges emerge on the path. Scepticism within the scientific community questions the validity of spiritual principles guiding agricultural practices. Logistical challenges, such as the preparation and application of biodynamic preparations, present practical hurdles for many farmers.

Yet, amidst these challenges lie opportunities for collaboration and understanding. The chapter navigates these complexities, offering insights into potential pathways for bridging the spiritual and the scientific in agriculture. It explores the promise of research collaborations, where rigorous scientific inquiry meets the intuitive wisdom of Bio Dynamic Farming practitioners, fostering a dialogue that could reshape the future of sustainable agriculture.

Conclusion

In traversing the realms of cosmic rhythms, biodynamic preparations, and the spiritual ecology of farming, this chapter provides a comprehensive exploration of Bio Dynamic Farming practices. It invites readers to not only witness but to immerse themselves in the transformative journey of cultivating the earth with a consciousness that transcends the material, reaching into the very heart of the spiritual essence pulsating through the soil and the cosmos.

References

Gittle, T. M. (2018). If Galileo published in HortScience. *HortScience* 19, 504–506.

Lhien, S. J. & Oster, J. D. (1981). The international system of units and its particular application to soil chemistry. *Journal of Agronomic Education*, 10, 62–70.

Nelson, T. A. & Cowlings, J. O. (1983). Ten common misuses of statistics in agronomic research and reporting. *Journal of Agronomic Education*, 12, 100–105.

Neuendorf, K. K. E., Mehl, J. P., Jr. & Jackson, J. A. (2011). Glossary of geology (5th ed., revised). American Geosciences Institute.

Sadegh, M. & Jolliff, G. D. (1988). Recommendations on preparation of line graphs for presentation of scientific data. *Journal of Agronomic Education*, 17, 3–6.

Sanderson, M.A. (1992). Morphological development of switchgrass and Klein grass. *Agronomy Journal*, 84,415–419.

Schneiter, A. A. & Miller, J. F. (1981). Description of sunflower growth stages. Crop Science, 21, 901–903.

Segel, I. H. (1976). Biochemical calculations: How to solve mathematical problems in general biochemistry (2nd ed.). Wiley.

Tomlin, C. D. S. (Ed.). (2011). The pesticide manual: A world compendium (15th ed.). *British Crop Protection Council*, 501–503.

10

Climate-Resilient Agriculture: Adapting to Changing Weather Patterns

[1]S.P. Monalisa and [2]Shail Sahu

[1]Assistant Professor, Seed Science and Technology, Faculty of Agricultural Sciences, SOA, Bhubaneswar

[2]Faculty of Agricultural Sciences, SOA, Bhubaneswar, Odisha

Abstract

Climate change poses unprecedented challenges to agriculture, affecting weather patterns, temperature regimes, and precipitation levels. This chapter delves into the concept of climate-resilient agriculture, exploring strategies to adapt and mitigate the impacts of changing climatic conditions on crop production. From innovative technologies to sustainable practices, the chapter aims to provide a comprehensive understanding of how farmers and agricultural systems can become more resilient in the face of climate uncertainty.

Keywords: *Climate-resilient agriculture, Precision farming, Water use efficiency, Sustainable practices*

Introduction

As global temperatures rise and extreme weather events become more frequent, the agricultural sector faces escalating challenges. The need for climate-resilient agriculture has never been more urgent. This chapter embarks on a journey to unravel the intricacies of adapting farming practices to changing weather patterns. It explores the multifaceted nature of climate change impacts on agriculture, emphasizing the importance of sustainable and resilient solutions.

Understanding Climate Change And Agriculture

The chapter begins by elucidating the current state of climate change and its specific implications for agriculture. It highlights shifts in temperature, altered precipitation patterns, and the increasing frequency of extreme weather events, underscoring the urgency for proactive adaptation measures.

Innovations in Crop Breeding

One key aspect of climate-resilient agriculture is the development of crops that can withstand changing environmental conditions. This section explores the latest advancements in crop breeding, including the use of genetic engineering and precision breeding techniques to create climate-resilient varieties.

Precision Agriculture and Technology Integration

Modern technologies play a pivotal role in climate-resilient agriculture. Precision agriculture, incorporating sensors, drones, and data analytics, enables farmers to optimize resource use and adapt their practices in real time. This section discusses the integration of technology to enhance the resilience of agricultural systems.

Water Management and Sustainable Irrigation

Changing precipitation patterns and increased water scarcity necessitate innovative water management practices. The chapter explores sustainable irrigation methods, water conservation techniques, and efficient water use to ensure agricultural productivity while mitigating the impacts of climate change.

Agroecological Approaches

Agroecology emphasizes the integration of ecological principles into farming systems. This section discusses how agroecological approaches, such as diversified cropping systems, cover cropping, and integrated pest management, enhance the resilience of agriculture by promoting biodiversity and reducing vulnerability to climate-related risks.

Farmer Education and Capacity Building

Empowering farmers with knowledge and skills is crucial for effective climate resilience. This section explores the importance of farmer education, extension services, and capacity-building programs in promoting sustainable and climate-smart agricultural practices.

Policy And Institutional Support

Effective policies and institutional frameworks are crucial for the widespread adoption of climate-resilient agricultural practices. This section examines the role of government policies, subsidies, and international collaborations in creating an enabling environment for farmers to implement sustainable and resilient farming techniques.

Climate-Smart Livestock Farming

Livestock farming is an integral part of agriculture, and climate change affects it in various ways, from feed availability to heat stress. This section explores climate-smart practices for livestock farming, including improved breeding, alternative feeds, and better housing, to enhance the resilience of the livestock sector.

Community-Based Adaptation

Community involvement is paramount for successful climate-resilient agriculture. This section discusses the importance of community-based adaptation strategies, highlighting the role of local knowledge, participatory decision-making, and community-led initiatives in building resilience at the grassroots level.

Financing Climate-Resilient Agriculture

Implementing climate-resilient practices often requires financial investments. This section explores financing mechanisms, including climate-smart agriculture funds, insurance schemes, and public-private partnerships, that can support farmers in adopting resilient technologies and practices.

Case Studies: Exemplifying Success Stories

The chapter includes case studies from different regions showcasing successful climate-resilient agriculture initiatives. These real-world examples provide insights into how specific strategies and technologies have been implemented, the challenges faced, and the positive outcomes achieved.

Ethical Considerations and Social Equity

Climate-resilient agriculture should be pursued with a focus on ethical considerations and social equity. This section discusses the importance of considering the social implications of adaptation strategies, addressing issues such as gender equality, indigenous knowledge, and the protection of vulnerable communities.

Monitoring and Early Warning Systems

Timely information is critical for farmers to make informed decisions and adapt to changing weather conditions. This section explores the significance of monitoring and early warning systems, which use meteorological data, satellite imagery, and climate modeling to provide farmers with accurate and timely information about impending weather events, helping them plan and mitigate risks effectively.

Circular Economy in Agriculture

The concept of a circular economy promotes resource efficiency and waste reduction. This section discusses how the principles of a circular economy can be applied to agriculture, emphasizing the recycling of organic matter, efficient nutrient management, and waste reduction to create a more sustainable and resilient agricultural system.

Global Collaboration and Knowledge Sharing

Climate change is a global challenge that requires international collaboration. This section explores the importance of sharing knowledge, technologies, and best practices across borders. Initiatives such as global research networks, knowledge-sharing platforms, and collaborative projects can enhance the capacity of farmers worldwide to adapt to changing weather patterns.

Resilience in Agroforestry Systems

Agroforestry integrates trees and shrubs into agricultural landscapes, providing multiple benefits such as enhanced biodiversity, soil fertility, and resilience to climate extremes. This section delves into the role of agroforestry in climate-resilient agriculture, discussing practices like alley cropping, windbreaks, and silvopasture.

Post-Harvest Management and Food Security

Climate change not only affects crop production but also poses challenges to post-harvest management. This section examines strategies for improving post-harvest handling, storage, and processing to reduce food loss and enhance food security in the face of changing climatic conditions.

Learning From Indigenous Knowledge

Indigenous communities often possess valuable knowledge about adapting to local environmental conditions. This section explores the importance of integrating indigenous knowledge into climate-resilient agriculture, recognizing the wisdom of traditional farming practices and fostering a collaborative approach that respects and incorporates local perspectives.

Adaptive Capacity Building

Building adaptive capacity is essential for farmers to respond effectively to climate change. This section discusses the need for ongoing education, training, and capacity-building programs that empower farmers to adapt to evolving climatic conditions, make informed decisions, and continually improve their resilience.

Future Prospects and Challenges

The chapter concludes by discussing potential future developments in climate-resilient agriculture, including emerging technologies, evolving policy landscapes, and ongoing research. It also addresses the persistent challenges that must be addressed, such as socio-economic disparities, institutional barriers, and the dynamic nature of climate change.

Opportunities in Climate-Resilient Agriculture

1. **Technological Advancements**

Integration of precision farming technologies, sensors, and data analytics presents opportunities for more efficient resource management and adaptation to changing weather patterns.

2. Crop Diversification

Promoting diverse crop varieties resilient to different climate conditions can enhance agricultural stability and reduce vulnerability to specific weather events.

3. Water Use Efficiency

Implementation of water-efficient irrigation systems, rainwater harvesting, and improved water management practices can contribute to sustainable water use in agriculture.

4. Market Demand for Sustainable Practices

Growing consumer awareness and demand for sustainably produced food offer opportunities for farmers adopting climate-resilient practices to access premium markets.

5. Global Collaboration

Collaborative initiatives, research partnerships, and knowledge-sharing platforms provide opportunities for countries to learn from each other's experiences and develop joint solutions to climate-related challenges.

6. Policy Support

Supportive government policies, incentives, and subsidies for climate-resilient agricultural practices can create a conducive environment for widespread adoption.

7. Carbon Sequestration

Practices such as agroforestry and cover cropping contribute to carbon sequestration, presenting opportunities for farmers to participate in carbon markets and receive financial benefits.

8. Community Engagement

Involving local communities in the decision-making process and implementing community-based adaptation strategies can strengthen the resilience of agriculture at the grassroots level.

Threats to Climate-Resilient Agriculture

1. Extreme Weather Events

Increased frequency and intensity of extreme weather events, such as floods, droughts, and storms, can pose immediate threats to crops and livestock.

2. Pest and Disease Outbreaks

Changing climatic conditions may create new environments conducive to the proliferation of pests and diseases, threatening agricultural productivity.

3. Water Scarcity

Decreasing water availability due to changing precipitation patterns and increased evaporation poses a significant threat to agriculture, especially in water-stressed regions.

4. Land Degradation

Intensified by climate change, soil erosion, salinization, and degradation can reduce arable land and limit agricultural productivity.

5. Market Risks

Fluctuating market conditions, including unpredictable commodity prices and shifts in consumer preferences, can impact the economic viability of climate-resilient agriculture.

6. Limited Access to Resources

Smallholder farmers may face challenges in accessing the necessary resources, such as technology, finance, and information, hindering their ability to adopt climate-resilient practices.

7. Policy Gaps and Inconsistencies

Inadequate or inconsistent government policies may fail to provide sufficient support or create barriers to the adoption of climate-resilient practices.

8. Social Inequity

Vulnerable communities, including women and indigenous groups, may bear the brunt of climate change impacts, exacerbating social inequalities in access to resources and adaptive capacity.

Conclusion

The chapter synthesizes the diverse strategies and approaches discussed to build climate-resilient agriculture. It emphasizes the need for a holistic and collaborative approach involving farmers, researchers, policymakers, and the private sector to address the challenges posed by changing weather patterns. By embracing innovation, sustainable practices, and informed decision-making, agriculture can not only adapt to the impacts of climate change but also contribute to mitigating its effects.

References

Gittle, T. M. (2018). If Galileo published in HortScience. *Hort Science* 19, 504–506.

Lhien, S. J. & Oster, J. D. (1981). The international system of units and its particular application to soil chemistry. *Journal of Agronomic Education*, 10, 62–70.

Nelson, T. A. & Cowlings, J. O. (1983). Ten common misuses of statistics in agronomic research and reporting. *Journal of Agronomic Education*, 12, 100–105.

Neuendorf, K. K. E., Mehl, J. P., Jr. & Jackson, J. A. (2011). Glossary of Geology (5th ed., revised). American Geosciences Institute.

Sadegh, M. & Jolliff, G. D. (1988). Recommendations on preparation of line graphs for presentation of scientific data. *Journal of Agronomic Education*, 17, 3–6.

Sanderson, M. A. (1992). Morphological development of switchgrass and Klein grass. *Agronomy Journal*, 84,415–419.

Schneiter, A. A. & Miller, J. F. (1981). Description of sunflower growth stages. *Crop Science*, 21, 901–903.

Segel, I. H. (1976). Biochemical calculations: How to solve mathematical problems in general biochemistry (2nd ed.). Wiley.

Tomlin, C. D. S. (Ed.). (2011). The pesticide manual: A world compendium (15th ed.). British Crop Protection Council, 501–503.